WITHDRAWN

IT'S THE LAW!

PETS, ANIMALS, AND THE LAW

*A compilation of our nation's laws on pets and animals,
as well as the legal rights and responsibilities
of our pets, ourselves, and others.*

*If you own a pet or any kind of animal—
or if you just love animals—
you have needed, do need, and will need this book.*

Judge William J. Wynn

EL DORADO COUNTY LIBRARY
345 FAIR LANE
PLACERVILLE, CA 95667

Copyright © 2002 by Judge William J. Wynn

All rights reserved. No part of this publication may be reproduced or transmitted in any form or by any means, electronically or mechanically, including photocopying, recording, or by any information storage or retrieval system, without the prior written permission of the publisher.

Published by Doral Publishing, Sun City, Arizona
Printed in the United States of America.

Copyedited by MaryEllen Smith
Interior design by The Printed Page
Cover by Masterpiece Publishing

Library of Congress Card Number: 2001094061
ISBN: 0-944875-72-6

Publisher's Cataloging-in-Publication
(*Provided by Quality Books, Inc.*)

Wynn, William J.
   It's the law! : Pets, animals and the law / William J. Wynn ; MaryEllen Smith (editor). -- 1st ed.
   p. cm. --
   Includes bibliographical references and index.
   LCCN: 2001094061
   ISBN: 0-944875-72-6

   1. Animal welfare--Law and legislation--United States--States--Popular works. 2. Domestic animals--Law and legislation--United States--States--Popular works. I. Smith, MaryEllen. II. Title.

KF3841.Z9W96 2001   344.73'049
                        QBI01-201154

CONTENTS

The Purpose of this Book · 1

Chapter One. Laws Protecting Animal Welfare and Recognizing
        Animal Rights · 13
  1-1.   Licensure of Pet Shops, Kennels and Breeders · · · · · · · · 14
  1-1a. Signs in Pet Shops · 15
  1-1b. Pet Shop Defined · 15
  1-2.   Necessity for Stringent Regulation of Pet Shops · · · · · · · 17
  1-2a. Pet shops; maintenance and care of premises and animals;
        definitions; punishment · · · · · · · · · · · · · · · · · · 18
  1-3.   Humane Method of Euthanasia; Services of Veterinarian
        Required: · 19
  1-4.   Pet Shops Required to Adequately House, Feed and
        Water Animals · 21
  1-5.   Pet Shops Forbidden to Sell to Animal Research Facilities · · 23
  1-6.   Pet Return Policy at Pet Shops · · · · · · · · · · · · · · · 24
  1-7.   Arbitration of Disputes Between Pet Shops and Purchasers · · 25
  1-7b. Rebuttable Presumption of Unfit Pet Sold · · · · · · · · · · 27
  1-8.   Number Restriction on Pet Owners · · · · · · · · · · · · · · 27
  1-9.   Pet Sitting Licensure · · · · · · · · · · · · · · · · · · · 31
  1-10. Cropping of Dog's Ears to be Performed by Veterinarian · · · 31
  1-11. US Public Law 91-579—The Animal Welfare Act · · · · · · · · 32
  1-12. Bans (Municipal) on Breeds of Dogs, Wolves, Wolf-hybrids · · 33
  1-13. Programs Requiring Greyhound Racing Facilities to Put
        Dogs Out For Adoption · · · · · · · · · · · · · · · · · · · 34
  1-14. Animal Therapy, Permitted at Health Care Facilities; Pet
        Therapy for Benefit of Patients · · · · · · · · · · · · · · 35
  1-15. Public Housing and Pet Ownership · · · · · · · · · · · · · · 36
  1-16. Pet Cemeteries · 38
  1-17. Pet Trust · 39
  1-18. Abandoned Wells to be Pet Secure · · · · · · · · · · · · · · 40
  1-19. Pets Protected Under Homestead Exemption · · · · · · · · · · 40
  1-20. Hospital and Medical Insurance for Pets · · · · · · · · · · 41

Chapter Two. Public Health, Safety, and Care · · · · · · · · · · · · · 43
    2-1.   Rabies Control; Definitions 44
    2-2.   Immunization; tags 46
    2-3.   Immunization; tag replacement. 46
    2-4.   Non-immunization; penalty 47
    2-5.   Pounds generally 47
    2-6.   Pounds; redemption or disposal of animals; lack of an
           immunization tag can result in euthanasia 48
    2-7.   Quarantine of animals 49
    2-8.   Animals exposed to rabid animal. 51
    2-9.   Impoundment, etc., of animals running at large on streets, etc. . 51
    2-10. Animal Research Facilities 52
    2-11. Housing accommodations for the blind with dog. 53
    2-12. Dog Guides. 53
    2-13. Definitions Related to Practice of Veterinary Medicine . . . 54
    2-14. "Grandfather clause". 56
    2-15. Abandoned animals. 57
    2-16. "Good Samaritan act;" emergency care. 57
    2-17. Tampering with racing animals prohibited 58
    2-18. Theft of property in the second degree 59
    2-19. Anti Obscenity Enforcement Act. 59
    2-20. Illegal to Use Animals in Certain Acts. 60
    2-21. Bear Wrestling 60
    2-22. Turtle Sales and Possession to be Strictly Regulated;
           Salmonella 62

Chapter Three. Dogs and Cats: · 65
    3-1.   Dogs and Cats to be Confined to Premises
           (Where County or City has Adopted this Provision) 66
    3-2.   Leash Laws 67
    3-3.   Pet Owner's Civil Liability for Injury, Damage or Death to
           Animals (Committed by Dog–Not Confined) 68
    3-4.   Pet Owner's Civil Liability to Guests, Licenses, Permittees;
           Trespassers; Persons on Owner's Property; Lawful Presence;
           Committed by Pet Confined 69
    3-4a. Specific classes of persons lawfully on owner's property in
           order to carry out duty 70
    3-4b. Nuisance. 71
    3-5.   Defenses Available to the Owner of the Pet in Civil Actions . 72
    3-6.   Pet Owners Criminal Liability for Causing or Allowing a
           Known Vicious or Dangerous Animal (Under His Control)
           to Injure or Destroy the Property, Persons or Pet of Another. . . 73

3-7. Pet Owners' Civil Liability for Injury, Damage or Death to Pets, Persons or Property Caused by Known Vicious or Dangerous Animal 75
3-8. Lawful Killing of a Dog or Other Animal for its Injurious Acts. 76
3-9. Rabid Pets, Owner's Liability.. 78
3-10. Prevention of Cruelty to Animals; Agencies and Enforcement Officers. 79
3-11. Neglected or Abused Animals; Care and Keeping by Humane Authority.. 80
3-12. Destruction of Abandoned Animals. 81
3-13. Cruelty to Animals—Criminal Penalties. 83
3-14. Title to Pets. 86
3-15. Dog Fighting. 86

Chapter Four. Barnyard Animals · · · · · · · · · · · · · · · · · · · **89**
4-1. Wanton or malicious injury, etc.; livestock.. 90
4-2. Wanton or malicious injury, etc., defenses. 90
4-3. Rail fences; cattle, horses, mules. 92
4-4. Barbed wire fences. 92
4-5. Definitions.. 92
4-6. Running at large; generally.. 93
4-7. Owner's liability. 94
4-8. Immunity of those involved in equine activities. 95
4-9. Use of sticks, whips, chains, etc., in livestock markets. . . . 95
4-10. Sale or purchase by dealers of cattle, hogs, etc., after sunset or before sunrise. 96
4-11. Estrays; generally.. 96
4-12. Notice of seizure—Lien for costs and damages.. 96
4-13. Staking Livestock on Highway Right of Way.. 97
4-14. Enforcement.. 97
4-15. Admissibility of certificate of registration in civil actions or criminal proceedings as to title or right of possession. 98
4-16. Furnishing, etc., of forms for registration, re-registration and transfer of brands by department. 98
4-17. Dipping of horses, mules or asses kept in tick infested lots, ranges, etc. 98
4-18. Transportation, etc., into state of ticky cattle, horses, mules, etc., prohibited. 99
4-19. County to Indemnify Owners of Cattle for Injuries Caused by Dipping. 99
4-20. Use of false or misleading advertising by public hatcheries and chick dealers or jobbers. 100

4-21. Rabbits and chicks, ducklings, or other fowl; sale, etc.,
as pets or novelties. 100
4-22. Feeding of garbage to swine.. 101
4-23. Possession, sale, etc. of hog cholera virus. 102
4-24. Keeping cockpit; cockfighting. 102
4-25. Underground stables. 102
4-26. Standards as to volume of air. 103
4-27. Transportation of Animals in Mines. 104
4-28. Enumeration of Conditions, etc., Constituting Public
Nuisances Menacing Public Health.. 104
4-29. Polluting Public Water Supply. 105
4-30. Persons riding animals or driving animal-drawn vehicles. . . 105
4-31. Uniform Certificate of Title Act. 106
4-32. Lien Declared: For Stud Services. 106
4-33. Lien on stock for pasturage or training. 107
4-34. Animal sales between sunset and sunrise 107
4-35. Choking, glanders, etc.; sale, etc., of afflicted horse or mule. 108
4-36. Mares or jennets subject to lien.. 108
4-37. Teeth of horse or mule; tampering. 109
4-38. Teeth of horse or mule; evidence of tampering. 109
4-39. Teeth of horse or mule; evidence of intent. 110
4-40. Teeth of horse or mule; transportation of animal in violation. 110
4-41. Brands and marks; unlawful imposition or alteration 110
4-42. Dead animals; disposal. 111
4-43. Depositing dead animals or fowl in running streams. 111
4-44. Duties generally; maintenance, inspection and copying
of reports of investigations of state toxicologist;
police authority of state toxicologist and assistants. 112

Chapter Five. Wild Animals—Their Protection · · · · · · · · · 113
5-1. Permits for collection of wild animals, birds, etc.,
for scientific purposes, etc. 114
5-2. Possession, sale, purchase, etc., of protected wild birds, etc. . . . 114
5-3. Enumeration of birds not protected. 115
5-4. Taking, etc., of protected birds or animals at night; taking, etc.,
of raccoons or opossums at night; taking of foxes at night. . 119
5-5. Hunting, etc., of or possession of protected birds or
animals during closed season. 120
5-6. Sale and purchase of game birds and animals including
the meat or other product thereof. 121
5-7. Hunting, etc., of wild turkeys with dogs. 122
5-8. Hunting, etc., of wild turkey hens, female deer, antelope
or elk, and unantlered male deer. 122

5-9.	Taking, etc., of deer from public waters.	123
5-10.	Taking, etc., of deer, antelope, moose or elk at night.	123
5-10a.	Protected Game: Antelope, moose, whitetail or mule deer, bear, elk, mountain lion, rocky mountain bighorn sheep, wild turkey, or subspecies—Hunting, selling, buying—Seizure of meat, head, hide or any part of animal by Conservation Officers.	124
5-11.	Taking, etc., of protected birds or animals by means of bait.	125
5-12.	Unlawful methods of hunting birds or animals protected by law or regulations.	126
5-13.	"Pen-raised quail" defined.	127
5-14.	Fowl to be hunted; minimum stock released for hunting.	127
5-15.	License required; rules and regulations.	127
5-16.	Hunting licenses required of preserve patrons; seven-day license; operators as agent vendors of licenses.	128
5-17.	Licenses on Weekends.	129
5-18.	Enforcement of game and fish laws; inspection of preserves.	129
5-19.	Definitions.	130
5-20.	Construction of article; purpose thereof.	130
5-21.	Stamp required for hunting migratory waterfowl; form; procedure.	130
5-22.	Issuance of stamp; cost; disposition of issuing fees.	131
5-23.	Dog trainer's license.	131
5-24.	When dogs permitted in areas; liability of owners of dogs at large in areas	132
5-25.	Impoundment of dogs; redemption or destruction of impounded dogs.	132
5-26.	Opening or closing of season for killing of beaver.	133
5-27.	Liability for injury or damage to persons or domestic animals of persons using traps, etc., to take, capture, etc., fur-bearing.	133
5-28.	Seizure, forfeiture and disposal of prohibited devices, etc., used in catching, killing, etc., fish or fur-bearing animals.	134
5-29.	Trapping on or from right-of-way of state highway.	135
5-30.	Checking of traps; hanging or suspending of bait over or within 25 feet of steel trap.	135
5-31.	Authority to prohibit importation of birds, animals, fish, etc.	135
5-32.	Release of turkeys into wild areas of state prohibited; exceptions; penalty.	138
5-33.	Wild Animals Are the Property of the State.	138
5-34.	Means of catching game fish generally.	141
5-35.	Catching game or Non game fish by use of gill, trammel, etc., nets.	141

5-36. Use of game fish for bait—Generally. 142
5-37. Same—Use of sunfish. 142
5-38. Laws Protecting Black Bass, Salmon, Walleye, Pike,
Trout and Lake Trout.. 143
5-39. Catching, etc., of fish in private ponds, lakes, pools or
reservoirs. 144
5-40. Saltwater Species. 144
5-41. Tax on terrapins caught, etc., for commercial purposes;
minimum legal size; possession of undersized terrapins. . . . 145
5-42. Crab catcher: license for use of more than five crab traps;
rules and regulations. 145
5-43. Authority and procedure for leasing of bottoms in
natural oyster reefs; cancellation and forfeiture of leases;
disposition of proceeds from leases. 146
5-44. Inspection of oyster beds; closure order; relay of oysters from
closed areas; promulgation of rules; penalty; enforcement. . . 146
5-45. Definitions, as respects Alabama, Georgia, Florida,
Mississippi, Louisiana, South Carolina and Texas.. 147
5-46. Minimum weight of shrimp taken, etc., for commercial
purposes; possession, sale, etc., of nonconforming shrimp. . . 148
5-47. Hardship gill net license; renewal and transfer. 149
5-48. Live bait shrimp dealers license. 150
5-49. Catching, etc., of shrimp; place and time.. 150
5-50. Catching, etc. of shrimp by persons with recreational
boat shrimping license; manner of taking; limitation on
quantities taken.. 150
5-51. Rivers, bayous and creeks permanently closed; areas
designed as exclusive bait shrimping areas. 151
5-52. Lobster—Maine or Spiny 151
5-53. Charge for buying or otherwise obtaining freshwater
mussels; disposition of revenues; violation as a misdemeanor. 153

Epilogue · 155

Glossary · 163

Statutes · 175

Index · 181

INTRODUCTION

The Purpose of this Book

As a trial judge for a quarter of my life, a stringent set of rules of behavior called the Judicial Canons of Ethics governed my activities, my associations and the very objects and depths of my friendships. The pervasive standard was neatly summed up in the admonition to "avoid even the appearance of impropriety."

Like my brother judges, I belonged to no clubs, restricted my social engagements, and bore confidences that I guarded by keeping mostly to my work. My work was my life; my fun was politics.

I was always the last to learn of fashion or fads. My children made great sport of my ignorance of the newest gadgets or latest Hollywood stars. Leonardo DiCaprio could have been Galileo's uncle for all I knew, and I never for a moment wavered in my choice of Kim Novak as the most beautiful actress in Hollywood.

So it was with the wonder and astonishment of Gomer Pyle, whose tag line was "Surprise! Surprise!," that I first saw a dog biscuit bakery at a local shopping center.

In an age where the needs of animals are, at last, beginning to be met, someone had chosen to minister exclusively to the wants of animals. And so it was that I began to recognize the emergence of a new type of care and affection that our society was finally beginning to bestow upon its earthly cotenants. My younger days had always been shared with animals, so the prospect that others were doing the same was warming and reassuring.

As a boy growing up fifteen miles outside of Birmingham, Alabama, my best friends were a rat terrier named Lady and a Tennessee walking horse named Dandy. Because both of my uncles were veterinarians, Santa Claus filled my stocking every year with such additions to a menagerie as a red squirrel, many rabbits, piglets, an alligator, an owl, a pen of Bob White quail, bobcats, feral cats, quarter horses, Arabian horses, Tennessee walkers, German shepherds, Danish Brown leghorns, mallard ducks, parakeets, a monkey, Labrador retrievers, a possum, a beaver, Jersey calves, miniature horses, and other such wonderful animals.

And so it was on that day, during my fiftieth year, I came to see that my love for animals was indeed a shared sentiment—imagine that, a dog biscuit bakery!

But how could I participate in this revolution? How could I, too, give back to these fascinating animals a measure of the companionship and the insight into existence that they've given me? I knew I couldn't bake biscuits—human or dog. I knew only the law, and the law had been a most jealous mistress.

That was it! I could research, write, and distribute a rudimentary Hammurabi's Code or Magna Carta on animals: their rights, the rights of their owners, the parameters of their proper nurturing, the boundaries of their conduct, and their intrinsic worth.

More than anything else, it would be written to and for people who love and care for animals—those customers of the dog biscuit bakery. It absolutely would not be written in the cryptic code of the law's practitioners, but rather in the easy give-and-take of information shared among people of kindred spirit.

My research initially focused on my own state of Alabama's laws regarding pets and other animals. Some of these laws were terribly antiquated, some surprisingly forward-thinking, and some so obscure and specific that I wondered if this were a situation peculiar to the Third World economy of a southern state where cotton had been king, or rather a common thread throughout our country. I believe that the tremendous number of laws on animals was equaled only by the number of statutes on intoxicating liquors—a characteristic of the old white-fisted, teetotaling Bible Belt.

To satisfy my curiosity, I began to research and compare laws on pets and animals in other states. After having completed *Pets,*

Animals, and the Law of Alabama, I soon realized that my curiosity about animal law had inspired another work that would be national in scope.

It was at this juncture that I raised my head, looked about, and wondered if other writers had covered this field. My research revealed that of some nine or ten treatments of the subject, five were legal casebooks, written by lawyers for lawyers. This had never been my vision. Of the four or five other books on animals and the law, three were discourses or court cases about only dogs or only cats, and the remaining works paraphrased and generalized various decisions of trial courts. Attempting to interpret or paraphrase a carefully worded court opinion is a dangerous undertaking.

So I discovered that the market I wished to reach had been uniquely overlooked. Surely there must be pet owners and other animal lovers who desire the veracity and authority of being presented with an actual legislative or judicial text, but need a common sense explanation and application of the meaning and effect of the legal principles. As a trial judge, I had spent years "charging" juries on the law they were to apply to the facts of a case, as well as the effect of that law. My goal of getting this message to my readership fit as comfortably as an old shoe.

At this point, I think it necessary and proper to declare the scope of this work. The core predicate of my research consists of those laws affecting the health, welfare, and safety of animals and people; laws regarding the duties of owners to animals; and laws concerning third parties and the public at large. Also included are laws forbidding certain animal activities and behaviors, laws regarding the propagation and health of various species, as well as the legal duties of persons interacting with animals through commerce or fortuity.

Thus, this book consists of important or needful laws common among most or all of the fifty states. It is important to point out that this work purposefully omits incidental laws, such as those relating to tax revenues, the labeling of animal feeds, or health department regulations concerning the offering of horse meat for human consumption, and the like. However, statutes or laws that I found particularly ingenious, peculiar, or obsolete are included for contrast. Exemplary statutes are given in text and striking contrasts are pointed out.

Simply stated, the scope of this work is not intended to be encyclopedic nor to be a codification of fifty codifications of the law. It is intended to intelligently inform and equip the reader with an awareness of the law as it relates to the animals in his or her life. The material is intended be read and enjoyed, not labored through like a listing of court decisions referenced like a telephone book.

By inference, the thousands of existing municipal ordinances among our nation's cities are referenced generally where clarity requires their mention. Significant federal legislation is covered. International laws are largely beyond the scope of this work. For instance, the quarantine of animals traveling to England, the quarantine of certain exotic animals imported into the United States, and the sundry treaties forbidding the trafficking or possession of ivory, sea turtle carapaces, green crocodile hides, or duck meat from China are not endlessly discussed.

This is not a book about animal rights, but because that most worthy subject is singularly crucial and deserving of a treatment in its own right, it is necessarily and often addressed where appropriate.

Much in the way I completed, then abandoned, *Pets, Animals, and the Law of Alabama* in favor of a work national in scope, to assume that this book or any book in such a rapidly developing area could ever be considered the last word is sheer folly.

During the last six months of cutting and pasting these materials, some legislatures across the country have passed animal protection laws so strong and proactive that opponents have declared them unconstitutional. In some cases, battle lines have been drawn; for instance, regarding the recreational killing of bighorn sheep, and the insistence of Japan and Iceland that whale populations need thinning.

Yet, in other instances, swords and shields have been laid by the riverside in a common pile. For example, both sides agree that salmon and cod have simply disappeared from waters off Newfoundland; motels across the US and Canada promote themselves as pet friendly; and the rate of pet ownership has soared among single women aged twenty to twenty-four, in direct proportion to their representation among the general population. Incidentally, of all pet owners surveyed, only seven percent report that protection is their primary motive for pet ownership. Seventy-nine percent cited companionship and affection as the impetus for owning a pet.

I believe the reader will find this book comprehensive and thorough. I hope that the population's dynamic attitude toward animals as fellow sojourners along life's road will continue to engender proposals of increasingly humane animal laws. If this hope is fulfilled, my work will have only just begun.

Prologue

From our parent country of England, we Americans, together with our Canadian neighbors, have taken what amounts to the bedrock of our law today. This body of law from England is called the common law.

However, as each state or province enacted its own statutes on a host of subjects, the legislatures tracked and improved upon, the common law, as well as the laws of the original thirteen states.

While forty-nine of the fifty states draw, primarily, on the common law of England, there is one notable exception: Louisiana, once the jewel of the French territories in North America, came into statehood with the civil law of France as the basis for its jurisprudence.

The civil law of France is best known for its emphasis on the sole fact that an individual had broken the law of the sovereignty, not the gravity or heinousness of the crime itself. French novelist Victor Hugo decried the harshness and improvidence of such a system in *Les Miserables*, in which Jean Valjean served twenty years for the theft of a loaf of bread that would feed his starving child.

A number of western and southwestern states were once occupied by the Spanish Conquistadors (prior to the Treaty of Guadeloupe Hidalgo, which ceded California, Texas, and New Mexico to the US), and so the law of Spain (and Mexico) prevailed in these regions. This body of law has had substantial impact on questions of water and riparian rights, watering rights for animals, and irrigation. Such laws have resurfaced recently in court disputes involving water rights for the cities of Los Angeles and Las Vegas. Divorce laws in some western states still draw from Spanish jurisprudence the concept of community property, in which spouses' separate estates are called *Gananciales*.

Range laws governing the vast expanses lying within the boundaries of western states have their genesis in both the aridity and the enormity of grazing lands. The Federal Range Code for Grazing Districts, enacted by the Bureau of Land Management Office, proscribed much of the law concerning the rights and liabilities of animals and their owners.

North America began as an agricultural society in which animals provided the labor to till the soil, the foodstuffs to fill the stomach, and the hides to warm the body. But cows or pigs wandered into the cornfields of neighboring farmers. Animals became lost or were rustled away. Old nags were curried and combed, then sold as fine, docile steeds. Because of such incidents, a voluminous body of law on animals came into being in order to keep the peace and provide judicious remedies for disputes among neighboring farmers. Initially, as colonies and territories became states, there was some commonality among the state statutes and codes pertaining to animals. The law of the market place and the inherent rights incidental to ownership were responsible for most animal-related law.

Then, an aspect of legislation (along with improved communication) emerged that allowed advances in animal-related legislation in one state to engender similar legislation in others. Each state has the equivalent of a legislative reference service. This is a civil service body of lawyers and persons proficient in law, syntax, and language. This service takes the legislature's version of a bill and creates an intensively researched proposal which, in theory, refines the wording of a law into what the law is intended to say.

These legislative reference services interact with like services in other states. Thus, when one finds a visionary statute on minimum hygiene requirements for pet shops in Ohio, it will not be unusual to find an almost identically worded statute in another state. This commonality among states, as well as uniform Federal laws such as the Animal Welfare Act, has caused all fifty states to have a surprising parity of important legislation.

From a millennium plus seven centuries of experience reconciling matters arising out of man's coexistence with the animal kingdom, the English devised a basic system of classification. Animals were and are divided into one of two broad classifications: *ferae naturae* and *domitae naturae*.

The former classification, *ferae naturae*, refers to animals of a wild nature, including bears, wolves, lions, tigers, and almost the complete host of Noah's passengers not normally found in a barnyard or parlor. The latter classification, *domitae naturae* (which yields the term domesticated), refers generally to farm animals and pets that have befriended or assisted humankind at least since the time of the Egyptian pharaohs. This grouping includes dogs, cats, oxen, cattle, horses, and the like. One distinguishing characteristic is the nature of the beast. Cows, cats, dogs, and horses are, by their nature and history, predominantly docile and willing, if not eager, to be trained or taught.

The random elephant, tiger, monkey, or python that is ostensibly comfortable around mankind still bears within its breast a wild nature and thus, even if it is considered domesticated or has been trained to be docile, remains prima facie (on the face of it) *ferae naturae*. Thus, it or its owner is deemed absolutely liable for any injury or damage inflicted by the animal.

In contrast, an animal in the *domitae naturae* classification, should it inflict damage or injury, only causes its owner to be liable if it has previously displayed vicious or destructive behavior. (Hence, while the owner is placed under a duty to "know" the animal's propensities, the animal is entitled to one "free bite" before its disposition can be considered bad.) On this broad classification of animals are structured the statutes and laws discussed in this book.

The last half of the twentieth century witnessed a cry for rights: consumer rights, children's rights, civil rights, and animal rights, to name but a few. It was probably the Kennedy administration's attention to African-Americans' dearth of rights that raised the consciousness of all oppressed peoples whose voices had been dinned to a whisper.

We live in an age of first impression. Husbands sue wives for child support; children go to court to acquire a legal separation from their parents; students sue universities for failing to equip them with a competitive edge in their academic specialty.

This same extreme swing of society's pendulum has finally allowed animals to have the functional equivalent of a nationwide seeing-eye dog. People operating within the light of sensitivity, rather than the dark specter of selfishness, have become vocal proponents and protectors of animals. Newspaper headlines commonly report stories of daring animal rescues. Over ten thousand motels now proudly advertise that they welcome pets. Hospitals have cats and dogs on staff to cheer up their patients. Animal-rights legislation grows steadily in terms of worthwhile purpose and frequency.

Is all this a fad or, at last, a recognition? It is unquestionably a recent but clear and strong recognition. Fads are not shored up by protective legislation. It has finally been recognized that animals are not mere brutes whose services and sinews may be gathered like honey from bee hives.

This compilation is designed to bring the reader through the recent, if belated, development of the law concerning animals. Further, the text of the various laws, successively progressive, demonstrates the response of lawmakers to the mandate of the people.

This work is meant to address laws common to most or all states on noteworthy and pertinent subjects. The subjects addressed are those currently in the national focus. It is from the character of the laws and subjects covered in this book that assessments of the strength and universality of animal-related legislation may be made in an informed and intelligent manner.

The assemblage of the information into five chapters, categorized as they are, is not meant to reflect the light of genius. It is simply a practical and original method of presenting a myriad of diverse, yet similar, topics.

Additionally, the final revision of this book omits the device of footnoting, which had pockmarked each paragraph of earlier versions. I do not wish to oblige readers to search for completeness. Case citations, titles, jurisdictions, reversals, parties, and dates have been omitted, where possible, in order to give the reader an uninterrupted flow of reliable information gleaned from similar statutes throughout the fifty states. A glossary of unfamiliar terms has been included for the reader's convenience.

CHAPTER ONE

LAWS PROTECTING ANIMAL WELFARE AND RECOGNIZING ANIMAL RIGHTS

"...Celts at that time trained their dogs to proceed in advance of their infantry and hurl themselves on the enemy who would use up their spears on them and become demoralized."

Who Were the Celts? Kevin Duffy

The topics of protective legislation covered in this chapter are the manifest evidence of laws enacted to protect pets and other animals in situations that almost all of us are likely to encounter. Buying a pet, going shopping in a mall, visiting someone in the hospital, or renting an apartment are among the dozens of common activities in which the effect of animal-related legislation is evident.

Legislatures are not usually moved to action by the needs of animals, but rather by the demands of persons who recognize the needs of animals. Lawmakers probably didn't pass laws intended to be conspicuous to their constituents, but it was in these areas of the public domain that an increasing awareness of animal rights first manifested itself. The topics presented here represent thoughtful, necessary mandates in a civilized society.

1-1. Licensure of Pet Shops, Kennels and Breeders

All states, thankfully, have statutes requiring pet shops, kennels, and pounds to be licensed by the state. Counties and cities have licensure requirements as well, but these are primarily for the purpose of raising revenue as opposed to setting minimum standards of care, health, and hygiene.

A typical statute provides that "No person shall maintain a pet shop until he has obtained from the commissioner a license to maintain such pet shop under such regulations as the commissioner provides, as respects sanitation, disease and humane treatment of animals and the protection of the public safety."

For purposes of comparison, another state's law declares that "No person shall procure any dog or cat for the purpose of resale unless such person holds a pet shop license under section 22-344. Any person who violates the provisions of this section shall be fined not more than one thousand dollars or imprisoned not more than one year, or both."

> At this juncture, I wish to assure the reader that hundreds of violators of such clearly worded statutes have claimed,

and will continue to claim, that the law was "vague" or they didn't think it "applied to me."

1-1a. Signs in Pet Shops

The licensure and humane treatment of pets, which states demand of pet shops, includes a requirement that conspicuously placed signs accompany the cages of pets certifying the breed, date of birth, parentage, registration (if applicable), and veterinary certificate of health. Almost all states require such signage in pounds or animal adoption agencies as well.

"A sign measuring not less than three inches in height and not less than five inches in width shall be posted on the cage of each dog offered for sale in a pet shop. The sign shall contain information, printed in black lettering on a white background listing the breed of such dog, the locality and state in which such dog was born, and any identification number of such dog as listed on the official certificate of veterinary inspection."

Do people read signs? It depends on what the sign says. If it calls attention to something free, it seems to glow like neon. If it warns of a requirement or prohibition, people swear its letters were in invisible ink.

If one finds oneself in a shop with no signs, I recommend a hasty retreat to a legal pet shop.

1-1b. Pet Shop Defined

States have generally defined a pet shop owner or pet shop operator as "any person who sells, offers to sell, exchange, furnish or offers for adoption dogs, cats, birds, fish, reptiles, amphibians or other pets or animals normally maintained in or near the household of the owner."

> Not too many years ago, pets and the other animals enjoyed little more protection than a "pet rock." Remarkably, a pet rock (or weather rock) has a place in our society. Such "pets" are appropriate for folks who can't seem to remember to water or feed a dog or cat.

One interesting statute on this topic reads as follows: "'Pet shop' means a place or vehicle in or on which dogs, cats, rodents, reptiles, fish, pet birds exotic birds or exotic animals not born and raised on those premises are kept for the purpose of sale to the public."

> I use this definition of pet shop to illustrate how some occurrence or incident peculiar to one state often winds up being specifically alluded to in a statute passed at a later time. In this case, a pet shop can be a vehicle. Was some quasi genius found to be peddling pets out of an old Good Humor truck? Probably, but the get-away-car-like appearance of this vendor should alert purchasers that what is here today might likely be gone tomorrow.

What is not a pet shop? Most states specify that "hobby breeders or individuals may not produce or transfer more than [a certain number, usually] two litters or more than 24 pet animals" without being subject to licensure—either as a pet shop or breeder. The bottom line, however, is that transfer of less than a statutory minimum of animals relieves one of compliance.

The definition of "pet" is probably given in at least thirty minutely different ways among the fifty states. Amazingly, all arrive at the same meaning, which is that a pet is "Every sentient creature" or "any domesticated animal normally maintained in or near the household of the owner thereof."

> The definition of "animal" under typical legislative wording is that of a "non-human creature; beast or brute." What a misinformed inaccuracy! I can truly say that in

> my fifty years of having animals as companions and partners, I have never known one to be a beast or a brute. Among the smartest creatures of any species I know is a half-bobcat who shares my bed and my heart on a daily basis.

1-2. Necessity for Stringent Regulation of Pet Shops.

The following statute, passed in 1987, best describes the need for regulation: "Emergency clause provided: It is hereby found and declared that abuses exist within the pet store industry regarding selling sick and injured animals to the public; failing to provide consumer guarantees for these animals consistent with status as companions; failing to provide appropriate time for the animals outside of cages for healthful exercise and socialization; failing to provide proper veterinary care; maintaining unsanitary and otherwise unhealthful conditions; and inhumane methods of killing sick and unwanted animals, and animals returned for failure of guarantee; that this act is designed to minimize or eliminate such abuses and should be given effect immediately. Therefore, an emergency is hereby declared to exist, and this act being necessary for the immediate preservation of the public peace, health, safety and welfare, shall be in full force and effect from and after the date of its passage and approval."

> Notice the use of the terms "companions" and "socialization," which demonstrate that the needs of animals extend well beyond just food and water. More importantly, public awareness of these higher needs is recognized. This is a good law. This statute and similar ones caused other states to follow, resulting in long overdue attention to be focused on pet shops.

> A typical statute on minimum standards in pet shops resulting from the universal recognition of the abuses in the industry is given below.

1-2a. Pet shops; maintenance and care of premises and animals; definitions; punishment

It shall be unlawful for any person who operates a pet shop to fail to do all of the following:

(1) Maintain the facilities used for the keeping of pet animals in a sanitary condition.

(2) Provide proper heating and ventilation for the facilities used for the keeping of pet animals.

(3) Provide adequate nutrition for, and humane care and treatment of, all pet animals under his care and control.

(4) Take reasonable care to release for sale, trade, or adoption only those pet animals which are free of disease or injuries.

(5) Provide adequate space appropriate to the size, weight and specie of pet animals.

(b) As used in this section:

(1) "Pet animals" means dogs, cats, monkeys, and other primates, rabbits, birds, guinea pigs, hamsters, mice, snakes, iguanas, turtles, and any other species of animals sold or retained for the purpose of being kept as a household pet.

(2) "Pet shop" means every place or premises where pet animals are kept for the purpose of either wholesale or retail sale. "Pet shop" does not include any place or premises where pet animals are occasionally sold.

(c) Any person who violates any provision of this section is guilty of a misdemeanor and is punishable by a fine of not to exceed one thousand dollars."

> Of course, any laxity in the self-regulation or enforcement of any of the above conditions can result in the establishment of a substandard puppy mill or kennel,

> either of which can subject animals to inhumane abuse and neglect.

1-3. Humane Method of Euthanasia; Services of Veterinarian Required:

Humane methods of and justifiable reasons for euthanizing pets and animals are required of pet shops and kennels or breeders. The services of a licensed veterinarian, a diagnosis, and a justifiable reason to euthanize an animal are almost always required. Some states permit a person of "caring and humane disposition, experienced in proper practice" to perform the euthanization.

Euthanasia of animals by pet shops

"(a) Euthanasia of any warm-blooded animal which was offered for sale by a pet shop and not sold or transferred to another owner shall be by lethal injection of sodium pentobarbital administered by a veterinarian licensed in this state or a person under his supervision.

(b) The commissioner shall revoke the license issued under section 22-344 of any pet shop that violates subsection, (a) of this section."

Most states specify the use of an "overdose of a central nervous system depressant." About half the states specify sodium pentobarbital as the vehicle for overdose.

Quizzically, Pennsylvania's statute sets out the standard humane method of overdose by a licensed veterinarian, yet the statute goes on to state the following: "Authorized method. Nothing in this act shall prevent a person or humane society organization from destroying a pet animal by means of firearms."

> In rural areas, unwanted pets are often simply dropped not too far from a dwelling by thoughtless persons. Sadly, these creatures often die of starvation or are shot as strays. Laws that provide for euthanasia or set up pounds and shelters make such acts of abandonment unnecessary.

Food Animals

> While driving in the waterfront area of Mobile, Alabama, in 1970, my attention was drawn to a fluttering movement at the open end of a building. To my amazed horror I saw an assembly line of white chickens, each hung upside down from a moving conveyor. As each chicken reached a gloved man stationed on the line, he would slash its neck with a knife, causing each passing animal to jerk and flutter as it bled out. I later learned that an electric charge in the knife blunted the animal's reflexes, causing it not to flutter as much.

> To my mind, this was inhumane and barbaric. Many states, however, now require humane methods of slaughtering food animals. One method is to quickly sever the carotid artery, which allegedly causes instantaneous anemia of the brain and painless death.

"All cattle, calves, horses, mules, sheep, swine, goats, or poultry shall be slaughtered by either of the following prescribed methods:

> (a) The animal shall be rendered insensible to pain by a captive bolt, gunshot, electrical or chemical means, or any other means that is rapid and effective before being cut, shackled, hoisted, thrown, or cast, with the exception of poultry which may be shackled.

> (b) The animal shall be handled, prepared for slaughter, and slaughtered in accordance with ritual requirements of the Jewish or any other religious faith that prescribes a method of slaughter whereby the animal suffers loss of consciousness by anemia of the brain caused by the simultaneous and instantaneous severance of the carotid arteries with a sharp instrument.

> This section does not apply to the slaughter of spent hens and small game birds, as defined by the department by regulation."

1-4. Pet Shops Required to Adequately House, Feed and Water Animals

A. A pet dealer shall do the following:

1. Maintain facilities in which cats or dogs are housed in a sanitary condition.

2. Provide cats or dogs with potable water and adequate nutrition.

3. Provide adequate space that is appropriate to the age, size, weight, species and breed of cat or dog. For the purposes of this paragraph, 'adequate space' means sufficient space for the cat or dog to experience normal body movements without having to make contact with the sides or top of the enclosure, including the ability to stand up, sit down, turn about freely and relax in a natural position.

4. If cats or dogs are housed on wire flooring, provide a resting board, a platform, or another similar device that is maintained in a sanitary condition and that allows the cat or dog to rest off the wire flooring.

5. If a cat or dog is afflicted with a contagious disease, handle the cat or dog in a manner that is required by S 44-1799.01, subsection B.

6. Promptly provide appropriate veterinary care when it is necessary.

B. A pet dealer shall not offer for sale a cat or dog that is less than eight weeks old.

C. A pet dealer who violates subsection A of this section is guilty of a class 1 misdemeanor."

> This is an example of common legislation among the states. Not only does it specify the requirements for adequate housing, feeding, watering, and sanitary maintenance, it also requires that animals kept in wire cages be provided a platform upon which to rest comfortably. This statute, as most others, requires space sufficient for the animal to stand, turn, and stretch out with adequate freedom of movement. The old stunt of thirty college students cramming themselves into a phone booth was roughly equivalent to the way animals were stuffed into cages at some pet shops and kennels.

Another state's requirements are somewhat more stringent:

Pet shops; maintenance and care of premises and animals; definitions; punishment

"It shall be unlawful for any person who operates a pet shop to fail to do all of the following:

(1) Maintain the facilities used for the keeping of pet animals in a sanitary condition.

(2) Provide proper heating and ventilation for the facilities used for the keeping of pet animals.

(3) Provide adequate nutrition for, and humane care and treatment of, all pet animals under his care.

(4) Offer for sale only pet animals which are free of disease or injuries.

(5) Provide adequate space appropriate to the size, weight and species of pet animals.

(b) As used in this section:

(1) 'Pet animals' means dogs, cats, monkeys, and other primates, rabbits, birds, guinea pigs, hamsters, mice, snakes, iguanas, turtles, and any other species of animal sold or retained for the purpose of being kept as a household pet.

(2) 'Pet shop' means every place or premises where pet animals are kept for the purpose of either wholesale or retail sale. 'Pet shop' does not include any place or premises where pet animals are occasionally sold.

(c) Any person who violates any provision of this section is guilty of a misdemeanor and is punishable by a fine of not to exceed one thousand dollars ($1,000.00), or by imprisonment in the county jail for not more than 90 days, or by both such fine and imprisonment."

> Please note that fines and corporeal punishments are being enhanced, coast to coast, since more progressive states (e.g., California, Arizona, Hawaii, and Colorado) have taken the lead.

1-5. Pet Shops Forbidden to Sell to Animal Research Facilities

Statutes generally state that "(a) It is unlawful for a pet shop to knowingly give, sell, barter, furnish or otherwise transfer an animal to another person if the ultimate destination of the animal is for research or killing for dissection."

> In John Steinbeck's humorous novel *Cannery Row*, a fellowship of hobos routinely caught frogs that they would then sell to a laboratory. This activity made enough money to ensure the group a steady beer supply. In realistic contrast, there is a huge illegal market for research animals. Heartless thieves steal pets and collect strays, then sell them to research facilities. Prohibiting pet shops from contributing to this criminal behavior is one activity the law can effectively regulate. Another is to require research facilities to keep an account of sellers, their addresses, and the price paid per animal. Almost no laws, however, give our police the latitude they need to enforce such regulations.

1-6. Pet Return Policy at Pet Shops.

A few states have noteworthy examples of statutes concerning the return of purchased pets.

Section: 44-1799.05 Purchaser remedies for sale of unfit cats or dogs; requirements; exceptions:

"A. A cat or dog that is purchased from a pet dealer is considered to be unfit for sale if either of the following applies:

1. Within fifteen days after the purchaser takes possession of the animal, a veterinarian who is licensed pursuant to title 32, chapter 21, states in writing that in the veterinarian's opinion the cat or dog has become ill or otherwise symptomatic due to any illness, injury or other defect that existed in the animal before the purchaser took possession of the animal.

2. Within sixty days after the purchaser takes possession of the animal, a veterinarian who is licensed pursuant to title 32, chapter 21 states in writing that the animal has a congenital or hereditary condition that adversely affects the health of the animal or that requires or is likely to require hospitalization or non elective surgical procedures."

> These statutes generally require conspicuous notice by means of the posting of a sign, specifying (usually) a fifteen-day period within which the pet may be returned to the pet shop for a refund. Mandatory causes for refund include congenital defects or illness. Ordinarily, the services of a veterinarian must be engaged to verify the pet's condition. Reacceptance by the pet shop, with no refund given, is the procedure specified when no defect or disease can be diagnosed—and with good reason. Can you imagine forcing the dissatisfied purchaser of an animal, who discovers he doesn't want or like a pet, being required to take the pet home? Or—worse yet—imagine a pet

shop owner saying "Sorry, sir, your cat only exhibits three of the six symptoms of mad cow disease. Enjoy." Scenarios like these would only encourage the abandonment of such animals.

These are the legalities of returning a newly purchased pet—unwanted—to the pet shop. If I may digress, allow me to expand on the subject from a personal standpoint of compassion, not law.

When I was a boy, my family owned horses. Two of the horses were older when we bought them. They were both such beloved pets that my father didn't want the animals to die around us kids, so he sold each one as it became feeble. As it turned out, my father's attempt to spare us sorrow resulted in the most painful consequence imaginable. Within a week of the cartage of each horse to its new home, it was dead—of a broken heart. Our pain was enormous. We had lost both the horses and the companionship of their last years while selfishly disregarding their love for us. This woeful tale is not applicable to the good sense and practicality of the pet return policy, but is mentioned here to show that the feelings of animals are a reality the law has overlooked.

1-7. Arbitration of Disputes Between Pet Shops and Purchasers.

Arbitration is a legally recognized method for resolving disputes without the need for a court trial and all that would entail. For our purposes, the process goes like this: the dissatisfied purchaser of a pet chooses an arbitrator, the pet shop chooses an arbitrator, then those two arbitrators choose a third. After hearing the evidence, the dispute is decided by the binding vote of the panel of all three arbitrators.

Contested actions; procedures:

"A. If a pet dealer contests a demand for remedies, the pet dealer may require the purchaser to produce the cat or dog for examination by a veterinarian who is licensed pursuant to title 32, chapter 21, unless the cat or dog has died. The pet dealer shall pay the costs of examination.

B. If the purchaser and the pet dealer are unable to reach an agreement within thirty days after the pet dealer receives the veterinarian statement or the veterinarian receives the cat or dog for examination, whichever is later, the purchaser may file an action in a court of competent jurisdiction or the parties may agree in writing to submit to binding arbitration.

C. The prevailing party in the action shall be awarded reasonable attorney fees if the other party acted in bad faith in seeking or denying the requested remedy."

> The good side of arbitration is that it is usually less expensive than a jury trial and is decidedly quicker. As an institution, the inherent bad side of arbitration is that arbitrators are usually unknown to the consumer. It is only from prior employment in the industry—the consumer's adversary—that the arbitrators draw their experience. This state of affairs can be summed up by this old lawyer's adage: consider it a bad sign when you see the opposing counsel and the judge eating lunch together during a recess.

> Arizona and New York have meaningful and successful alternative dispute resolution statutes pertaining to pet shop—purchaser disagreements. Only a minority of other states have seen fit to provide specifically for arbitration in this area; all states, however, by virtue of federal law, provide for arbitration as a method of dispute resolution.

1-7b. Rebuttable Presumption of Unfit Pet Sold.

A presumption is the legal likelihood or probability of a fact. A rebuttable presumption is a fact presumed to be the case unless and until it is overcome by proof of absolute certainty (a proven fact) or a fact of greater probability.

> Some states, in legislating the mandated policy regarding animals returned to pet shops, have determined that a rebuttable presumption exists in favor of the customer, that is, that the pet was sick or genetically deformed at the time of sale. Of course, the veterinarian's examination may reveal that this was or was not the case. If the veterinarian were to diagnose something definitively and clearly genetic—say, hip dysplasia—this would constitute a conclusive presumption in favor of the customer. New York and Arizona have passed shining examples of this type of legislation.

> By inserting the rebuttable presumption into such situations, the issue is streamlined and requires only a veterinarian's examination.

1-8. Number Restriction on Pet Owners.

Laws among states seldom impose outright restrictions on the number of pets owned by individuals and hobby breeders. However, cities and counties readily step up to the plate and impose such restrictions in densely populated cities or multifamily residences.

Regarding kennels, commercial breeders, pet shops, and pounds, state laws provide restrictions that are only classifications of numbers of pets. Correspondingly higher fees are required as the number of animals increases.

The following excerpts are quite lengthy, but necessary to give the reader an idea of what to expect concerning numbers of pets and graduated fees.

"Kennel Class I. To keep or operate a private kennel, pet shop-kennel, research kennel, dealer kennel or breeding kennel for a cumulative total of 50 dogs or less of any age during a calendar year—$75.00 per year.

Kennel Class II. To keep or operate a private kennel, pet shop-kennel, research kennel, dealer kennel or breeding kennel for a cumulative of 51 to 100 dogs of any age during a calendar year—$200 per year.

Kennel Class III. To keep or operate a private kennel, pet shop-kennel, research kennel, dealer kennel or breeding kennel for a cumulative total of 101–150 dogs of any age during a calendar year—$300.00 per year.

Kennel Class IV. To keep or operate a private kennel, pet shop-kennel, research kennel, dealer kennel or breeding kennel for a cumulative total of 151 to 250 dogs of any age during a calendar year—$400.00 per year.

Kennel Class V. To keep or operate a private kennel, pet shop kennel, research kennel, dealer kennel or breeding kennel for a cumulative total of 251 or more dogs of any age during a calendar year—500.00 per year.

Boarding Kennel Class I To keep or operate a boarding kennel having the capacity to accommodate a total of 1 to 10 dogs at any time during a calendar year—100.00 per year.

Boarding Kennel Class II	To keep or operate a boarding kennel having the capacity to accommodate a total of 11 to 25 dogs at any time during a calendar year—$150 per year.
Boarding Kennel Class III	To keep or operate a boarding kennel having the capacity to accommodate 26 or more dogs at any time during a calendar year—$250.00 per year."

Another common restriction law is, again, a classification:

"(1) 'Animal shelter' means a public or private facility licensed pursuant to this article and the rules and regulations adopted pursuant thereto.

(1.5) 'Bird hobby breeder facility:' means any facility engaged in the operation of breeding and raising birds for the purpose of personal enjoyment that does not transfer more than thirty birds per year.

(2) 'Canine hobby breeder facility' means any facility which transfers no more than twenty-four dogs per year or breeds no more than two litters per year, whichever is greater.

(2.5) 'Commercial dog breeder:' means a dog breeder that transfers at least one hundred dogs per year, excluding racing greyhounds that are not intended to be companion pets."

> Kennels and breeders, as previously stated, encounter restrictions in the form of the cost of licensing, which is determined by the number of animals kept or transferred per year. Such establishments pay larger license fees and are subject to state laws regarding care and treatment. The form of abuse described as puppy mills, however, has not been adequately addressed or entirely forbidden. For instance, Pennsylvania and Colorado have licensing fees determined by animals numbering two hundred fifty—or more.

> Restrictions on the number of animals owned are so potentially odious as to threaten the rights of due process under the Fourteenth Amendment to the Constitution. There is, however, a worthy consideration within this debate of restrictions on numbers of pets and other animals. Can an owner of say, two hundred fifty German shepherds properly care for, observe, and nurture such a large number of creatures?

> The answer, of course, is yes! Under carefully worded and properly enforced inspection laws, the owner must afford the proper care and treatment. With farsighted inspection mandates, puppy mill abuses may be eliminated without the need for numerical restrictions.

Pets in Apartments

Apartment leases typically restrict the number of pets that may be kept on premises. Historically, landlords often forbade pet ownership, or required a deposit of such size that it effectively imposed a prohibition.

> America's growing demand for animal companionship has led to fairly standardized lease language that permits pet ownership upon payment of a reasonable pet or damage deposit. A few states mandate that such a deposit cannot exceed the amount of one month's rent. However, the same lease language requires that the pet (or pets) be kept upon the resident's leased premises (and on common areas when accompanied by the resident), that they not constitute a nuisance, and not annoy other residents or damage their property or leasehold.

1-9. Pet Sitting Licensure.

Most states are enacting legislation on pet sitting licensure (if they have not already done so). The licensure requirement is often seen as a method of collecting yet another occupational tax. However, it is also found under occupations exempted from carrying mandatory worker's compensation insurance. Arkansas, for example, acknowledges pet sitting in the following context:

> "(a) As used in this section, 'domestic labor' means any occasional, irregular, or incidental work related to and in or around private residences, including but not limited to baby-sitting, pet sitting, similar household chores, and manual yard work. This definition specifically excludes industrial homework, work for a third party such as a sitting service, and any activity determined by the Director of the Department of Labor to be hazardous pursuant to the provisions of Section 11-6-107(b)."

> Is a licensed but untrained sitter any safer for our pets than leaving the pet alone? Ideally, licensing would require the training, psychological evaluation, and aptitude testing of the applicant.

1-10. Cropping of Dog's Ears to be Performed by Veterinarian.

> The practice of cropping (or making pointed) the ears of Doberman Pinschers and other breeds in order to ensure that the ears stand up and give the animal the characteristic look of the breed must, by common sense alone, be done by a caring and trained professional. Similarly, the docking of a horse's tail must be performed by a veterinary professional. Connecticut's statute is a typical example of this law, and many other states classify cropping as a surgical procedure requiring the services of a veterinarian. It is regrettable that it takes a law to require humans to do for pets what good judgment and caring should demand.

"Whoever, not being a veterinarian duly registered under chapter one hundred and twelve, crops or cuts off the whole or any part of the ear of a dog shall be punished by a fine of not more than two hundred and fifty dollars. If a dog with an ear cropped or cut off in whole or in part and with the wound resulting therefrom unhealed is found confined upon the premises or in the charge or custody of any person other than such veterinarian, or a dog officer of a city or town duly appointed under section one hundred and fifty-one of chapter one, such fact shall be *prima facie* evidence of a violation of this section by the person in control of such premises or the person having such charge or custody."

1-11. US Public Law 91-579—The Animal Welfare Act.

The Animal Welfare Act is federal legislation that applies to all states of the Union. This is a sweeping set of laws that address interstate transportation and importation of animals. It proscribes minimum standards of care and sets forth laws on health and public safety regarding pets and other animals. Federal jurisdiction is permitted because animals, animal feed, and supplies are transferred via interstate commerce. Although people sometimes curse big government as oppressive and costly, the humane care and treatment of all animals is now a dream within reach due largely to federal intervention.

—USCA—7 USCA s 2131. Congressional statement of policy

"The Congress finds that animals and activities which are regulated under this chapter are either in interstate or foreign commerce or substantially affect such commerce or the free flow thereof, and that regulation of animals and activities as provided in this chapter is necessary to prevent and eliminate burdens upon such commerce and to effectively regulate such commerce, in order—

> (1) to insure that animals intended for use in research facilities or for exhibition purposes or for use as pets are provided humane care and treatment;

(2) to assure the humane treatment of animals during transportation in commerce; and

(3) to protect the owners of animals from the theft of their animals by preventing the sale or use of animals which have been stolen.

The Congress further finds that it is essential to regulate, as provided in this chapter, the transportation, purchase, sale, housing, care, handling, and treatment of animals by carriers or by persons or organizations engaged in using them for research or experimental purposes or for exhibition purposes or holding them for sale as pets or for any such purpose or use."

1-12. Bans (Municipal) on Breeds of Dogs, Wolves, Wolf-hybrids.

Thus far, bans on the possession or ownership of a particular breed of dog inevitably follow some news story about a vicious rottweiler or crazed pit bull. Action becomes reaction as the event is parlayed into a municipal law (which frequently garners votes for municipal officeholders).

Shortsightedness is the common denominator of all such local laws. All states, however, require the licensure of "vicious dogs," wolf-dog hybrids, coydogs, and canid and felid breeds (such as wild domestic cats or bobcats). Most states that address the subject of wolf-dog hybrids and known vicious dogs specify that the possession of such animals requires a special license.

Many states have statutes proscribing the lawful killing of such animals under specified circumstances, such as this one:

"Dangerous Dog—Belongs to a breed that is commonly known as a pit bull dog. The ownership, keeping, or harboring of such a breed of dog shall be *prima-facie* evidence of the ownership, keeping, or harboring of a vicious dog."

In contrast, Virginia's statute is the result of informed, intelligent information gathering prior to the passage of a measure that will have long-term consequences. In other words, an animal that has been *domitae naturae* for centuries will not become *ferae naturae* by the act of some legislature.

> "No canine or canine crossbreed shall be found to be a dangerous dog or vicious dog solely because it is a particular breed of canine or canine crossbreed. No animal shall be found to be a dangerous dog or vicious dog if the threat, injury or damage was sustained by a person who was (1) committing, at the time, a crime upon the premises occupied by the animals' owner or custodian, (2) committing, at the time, a willful trespass or other tort upon the premises occupied by the animal's owner or custodian or (3) provoking, tormenting, or physically abusing the animal, or can be shown to have repeatedly provoked, tormented, abused, or assaulted the animal at other times. No police dog which was engaged in the performance of its duties as such at the time of the acts complained of shall be found to be a dangerous dog or a responding to an injury, or was protecting itself, its kennel, its offspring, or its owner or owner's property, shall be found to be a dangerous dog or a vicious dog."

1-13. Programs Requiring Greyhound Racing Facilities to Put Dogs Out For Adoption.

Every state that allows pari-mutuel betting (and greyhound racing) is required to establish and promote a program to facilitate the adoption of retired greyhounds by the general public.

"The commission shall establish financial assistance procedures for promoting adoption of racing greyhounds as domestic pets. The provision of financial assistance to nonprofit enterprises for the purpose of promoting adoption of racing greyhounds as domestic pets is contingent on a finding by the commission that the program presented by the enterprise is in the best interest of the greyhound racing industry and this state. Upon a finding by the commission, the commission is authorized to make grants to nonprofit enterprises whose programs promote adoption of racing greyhounds."

> Under such legislation, the racing commission must provide funding for the adoption and public awareness programs, as well as for the maintenance and nourishment of the greyhounds for a minimum period during which adoption may occur. I have seen countless greyhounds retired from the track who are now loyal, well-trained companions—much too valuable a resource to be destroyed.

1-14. Animal Therapy, Permitted at Health Care Facilities; Pet Therapy for Benefit of Patients.

Whether called animal therapy or pet therapy, this legislation does more for animal rights than almost all other legislation combined. Statutory recognition of the therapeutic benefits of patient-animal interactions in hospitals and long-term health care facilities is insightful and compassionate. More and more oncology, cardiac, pediatric, and Alzheimer's units—as well as other inpatient areas—are keeping well-trained animals on their premises for the mutual physical, mental, and spiritual well-being produced by such encounters.

Pet therapy programs

"Use of pet therapy—Notwithstanding any inconsistent provision of law, rule or regulation to the contrary, and subject to the approval of the secretary, every health care facility may, at the discretion of the health care provider, invite a nonprofit organization or an individual to bring domesticated pets onto the premises of the facility or may board domesticated pets on the premises of the facility if the pet therapy would, in the determination of the secretary and the health care provider, tend to promote the general well-being of the residents of the facility. The secretary shall adopt rules and regulations necessary to implement the provisions of this act."

> States with such statutes are still in the minority, but include Pennsylvania, Arizona, Alabama, Hawaii, Florida, and California. Hawaii's statute allows a patient's own pet to visit, with staff permission.

Animal therapy

"Animals of the kind commonly kept as household pets may be brought into long term health care facilities for the purpose of visiting patients therein. The institution shall determine whether an animal is suitable for visitation, the location where the visit may take place, and the policies governing the visit. At the discretion of the institution, the animal owner may be required to produce written documentation from a veterinarian attesting to the animal's good health, before visitation is permitted."

> The interface between loyal, loving, non-judgmental animals and human patients has produced phenomenal results.

1-15. Public Housing and Pet Ownership.

"Elderly and handicapped tenants living in publicly-assisted rental accommodations are allowed pets in their housing units despite any prohibition in the lease. 'Pets' is qualified by number and subject to good behavior."

Pets for elderly and handicapped tenants; exceptions; conditions; appeal procedures; definitions.

"A. Notwithstanding any other statute, a public agency which owns, operates, manages or contracts for rental housing accommodations shall not prohibit elderly or handicapped tenants from keeping pets in their dwelling units.

B. This section does not prevent a public agency which owns, operates, manages or contracts for rental housing accommodations from requiring the removal of any pet which by its conduct or condition constitutes a threat or nuisance to other occupants of the housing project. A person shall not keep a pet in violation of health statutes or under circumstances constituting cruelty to animals as defined in Section 13-2910.

C. A public agency which owns, operates, manages or contracts for rental housing accommodations shall not impose any requirement which makes the keeping of a pet by an elderly or handicapped tenant financially prohibitive and shall not in any case require a deposit or more than one month's rent for the keeping of a pet. This section does not relieve an elderly or handicapped tenant from any liability otherwise imposed by law for damages caused by the tenant's pet."

> Other states make similar provisions for pets in public housing for the elderly or persons requiring supportive services.

"Notwithstanding any other provision of law, no public agency which owns and operates rental housing accommodations, shall prohibit the keeping of not more than two pets by an elderly person or person requiring supportive services in the rental housing accommodations."

> Connecticut, Washington, D.C., California, Arizona, Delaware, Kansas, and Minnesota have exemplary statutes regarding pets in public housing. Such statutes are gaining rapid acceptance in other states. Alaska and Alabama have no such statutes due to the rich and powerful landlord groups that lobby their legislatures.

> California allows pets in live-aboard marinas and mobile home parks, and prohibits charging a fee for pets if no common pet kennel is provided.

Pets in Mobile Home Parks:

"(A) A homeowner shall not be charged a fee for keeping a pet in the park unless the management actually provides special facilities or services for pets. If special pet facilities are maintained by the management, the fee charged shall reasonably relate to the cost of maintenance of the facilities or services and the number of pets kept in the park.

(B) If the management of a mobile home park implements a rule or regulation prohibiting residents from keeping pets in the park, the new rule or regulation shall not apply to prohibit the residents from continuing to keep the pets currently in the park if the pet otherwise conforms with the previous park rules or regulations relating to pets. However, if the pet dies or no longer lives with the resident, the resident does not have the right to replace the pet.

(C) Any rule or regulation prohibiting residents from keeping pets in the mobile home park shall not apply to guide dogs, signal dogs, or service dogs."

1-16. Pet Cemeteries.

> Currently, all states legally recognize the existence of pet cemeteries. Under the law, a perpetual trust must be set up (as is the case with all cemeteries) for the care and maintenance of the property. Most states restrict internment to household pets and exclude barnyard animals. Ohio has such a restriction.

1-17. Pet Trust.

Any trust involves the formation of a legal instrument set up for a specified period that provides that care and funding are to be administered to the objects specified in the trust. Typically, a bank or other fiduciary is named by the trustor (one who sets up, funds, and describes the beneficiaries and period of existence of the trust), and the fiduciary is charged with carrying out the purposes of the trust for the life or lives of the beneficiaries. For instance, such an instrument for pets may be worded like this: "For the nurturing care and maintenance of my cats and/or the surviving cat, for so long as they, or any of them, lives." About one-fourth of states have enacted statutes specifically allowing trusts to be set up for domesticated animals or pets. Alaska, Arizona, and Pennsylvania have such statutes.

> Other states do not prohibit a pet from being the beneficiary of a trust. However, in those states, the settlor or trustor (who wishes to create such a trust) must do so under general trust law. In such a situation, an "honorary duty" would be imposed upon the trustee to care for the animals.

Honorary trusts; trusts for pets; conditions.

"(A) If a trust is for a specific lawful non charitable purpose or for lawful non charitable purposes to be selected by the trustee and there is no definite or definitely ascertainable beneficiary designated, the trust may be performed by the trustee for not longer than twenty-one years whether or not the terms of the trust contemplate a longer duration.

(B) A trust for the care of a designated domestic or pet animal is valid. The trust terminates when no living animal is covered by the trust. A governing instrument shall be liberally construed to bring the transfer within this subsection, to presume against the merely precatory or honorary nature of the disposition and to carry out the general intent of the transferor. Extrinsic evidence is admissible in determining the transferor's intent."

1-18. Abandoned Wells to be Pet Secure.

All states require wells and similar traps to be filled or covered over so as to prevent accidental or purposeful entry by a pet, child, or other being.

Plugging, sealing or capping abandoned wells required—Rules.

"If the owner of an existing well drills a replacement well and if the owner has no plan to use the existing well, the existing well is considered abandoned. The well owner shall plug the abandoned well within thirty days after the new well is ready for use. Any well that is being used or is not considered abandoned shall be sealed or capped at the surface. The Water Management Board shall promulgate rules pursuant to chapter 1-26."

1-19. Pets Protected Under Homestead Exemption.

> Pets are legally considered the personal property of an owner, just as one may own a savings account, furniture, or clothing. Thus all states have laws exempting or setting aside a certain sum (consisting of money, personal property, and other personal items) that a person may keep or withhold from creditors in the case of bankruptcy, probate of an estate, or other legal process. Thus, one may keep any or all pets whose total value does not exceed the amount of the exemption. However, "pets" means and includes any animals held for noncommercial purposes and not as an investment.

> The personal effects, house hold furnishings, and pets of any person shall be exempt from taxation.

"The phrase 'personal effects, household furnishings, and pets' does not include boats, aircraft, vehicles, or personal property held or used in connection with a trade, profession, or business, or pets so held or used."

1-20. Hospital and Medical Insurance for Pets.

A typical statute in a fast-growing number of states provides that "Any insurer writing any coverage to which the provisions of Section 17-17-1 apply may offer group or individual policies or contracts which provide benefits for hospital and medical services for pets, provided that these services are provided by a veterinarian licensed pursuant to chapter 16 of Title 45 of the Revised Statutes or by the laws of any other state. The policy or contract may provide for exclusions or deductibles, or both. As used in this section, 'pet' means any domesticated animal normally maintained in or near the household of the owner thereof."

Chapter Two

Public Health, Safety, and Care

> *"She asked the cowhand to let her look after the cows, but he drove her away. Then she began going off for the whole day with the flock of her own accord...As she was of great use to the cowhand...he no longer drove her away..."*
>
> *The Idiot,* by Fyodor Dostoevsky

2-1. Rabies Control; Definitions.

"As used in this chapter, the following words and phrases shall have the following meanings respectively ascribed to them unless the context clearly indicates otherwise:

(1) CANINE CORPS DOG. Those members of the canine family maintained by governmental agencies for exclusive use in official duties assigned to those agencies. Seeing eye dogs shall be included within the meaning of this definition.

(2) CAT. All members of the domesticated feline (*Felis catus*) family three months of age or older.

(3) DOG. All members of the domesticated canine (*Canis familiaris*) family three months of age or older.

(4) EXPOSURE TO RABIES 'has been exposed.' Seized with the teeth or claws, so that the skin of the person or animal seized had been nipped or gripped, or has been wounded or pierced and includes suspected or confirmed contact of saliva with a break or abrasion of the skin or with any mucous membrane, as determined by a licensed physician.

(5) HEALTH OFFICER. The injection, in a manner approved by the State Health Officer and the State Veterinarian, of anti rabies vaccine approved by the State Health Officer and the State Veterinarian. The administration of anti rabies vaccine to species other than those for which reliable immunization data is available shall be a violation of this chapter.

(6) IMPOUNDING OFFICER. An agent of a county or municipality vested with impounding authority for animals covered under this chapter.

(7) OWNER. Any person having a right of property in the animal, or who keeps or harbors the animal, or who has it in his care, or acts as its custodian, or who permits the animal to remain on or about any premises occupied by him.

(8) PERSON. Individuals, firms, partnerships, and associations.

(9) QUARANTINE FOR RABIES OBSERVATION. Confinement under the direct care, custody, control, and supervision of a licensed veterinarian for a period of 10 days subsequent to the date of the exposure, or as otherwise directed by the State Health Officer."

> This is a most important section of the law in all states. Here's everything you could possibly want to know about rabies. The law lists those pets subject to the law (and susceptible to infection). It goes like this: "seized with the teeth or claws, so that the skin of the person or animal seized has been nipped or gripped or has been wounded or pierced and includes suspected or confirmed contact of saliva with a break or abrasion of the skin or with any mucous membrane, as determined by a licensed physician." In other words, any scratch or abrasion that is suspect should be examined by a physician. A puncture wound can close and saliva will dry. Only a physician's inspection can be trusted.

> It should be noted here that rabies remains one of the world's most feared and dreaded diseases. If undetected, it very nearly always results in a fatal outcome. The word rabies is derived from the Latin *rabies*, meaning "madness" or "rage." English history recounts an epidemic of rabies as early as 1026.

> Of course, all the topics in this section have served (and still serve) as various methods of controlling rabies.

2-2. Immunization; tags.

"Coincident with the issuance of the certificate of immunization, the rabies officer, his authorized representative, or any duly licensed veterinarian, who provided the certificate shall furnish a serially numbered tag bearing the same number and year as that of the certificate, which tag shall at all times be attached to a collar or harness worn by the dog or cat for which the certificate and tag have been issued."

> When the veterinarian or health officer issues the certificate of vaccination and records the number, he is also to issue a tag to be affixed to the dog or cat's collar or harness. In my home state of Alabama, people must be told this sort of thing. Otherwise, G. Beauregard O'Shea of Socapatoy, Alabama, might take delivery of the tag and forthwith bury it behind the chicken coop, near the silverware.

2-3. Immunization; tag replacement.

"In the event of tag loss when the same has been legally issued, every replacement thereof shall be upon such terms as may be agreed upon with the rabies officer or veterinarian by whom the animal has been immunized. In such instance, a new certificate marked 'duplicate' may be issued setting forth the number of the new tag and the certificate issued and distributed according to the preceding section.

If the tag is lost, upon a specified fee, the veterinarian or officer must issue a replacement tag denoted as 'duplicate.'"

> Incidentally, this numbered rabies tag has been the charm that has returned many a lost pet to its master.

2-4. Non-immunization; penalty.

"The owner of any dog or cat found not wearing the evidence of current immunization as provided herein or for which no certificate of current immunization can be produced, and which is apprehended by an officer or other person charged with the enforcement of this chapter, shall forthwith be subject to a penalty to be imposed by the rabies officer not to exceed an amount equal to twice the state approved charge for immunization, in addition to the fee heretofore prescribed for immunization. When collected, the said penalty shall accrue to the rabies officer or his agent, except in the case of a rabies officer employed full-time on salary, in which case the penalty shall accrue to the employing agency or agencies" (Unlawful removal of a rabies tag is theft).

> So, if any dog or cat is found not wearing a tag, and no certificate of immunization can be produced, the owner is subject to a fine not exceeding twice the cost of the original certificate. Note that the statute specifically states that "the said penalty shall accrue to the rabies officer." Does this mean that a penalty for breaking the law becomes a profit for the enforcer? Well, up until the twenties and thirties, sheriffs in counties, boroughs, or parishes throughout the country were allowed to keep the fines or penalties they collected in lieu of other compensation.

2-5. Pounds generally.

"It shall be the duty of each and every county in the state to provide a suitable-county pound and impounding officer for the impoundment of dogs and cats found running at large in violation of the provisions of this chapter. Every municipality with a population over 5,000 in which the county pound is not located shall maintain a suitable pound or contribute their pro rata share to the staffing and upkeep of the county pound. When dogs and cats are impounded and if the owner then is known, such owner shall be given direct notice of the impoundment of said animal or animals belonging to him."

> Thus, every county must, by law, have a pound. If a municipality with a population over five thousand has no pound, it is to set up an acceptable place for boarding animals to be kept or disposed of under this section.

> As a child, I lived in an urban neighborhood where no one had fences, and so our pets ran at large. When a prepubescent voice shouted "Dog Catcher!" housewives in a hundred homes would discover Junior and Fido, fleas and all, suddenly watching TV in the living room.

2-6. Pounds; redemption or disposal of animals; lack of an immunization tag can result in euthanasia.

"All dogs and cats which have been impounded for lack of rabies immunization in accordance with the provisions of this chapter, due notice of which shall have been given to the owner as provided in the previous section, may be humanely destroyed and disposed of when not redeemed by the owner within seven days. In case the owner of an impounded dog or cat desires to make redemption thereof, he may do so on the following condition: He shall pay for the immunization of the animal and the penalty as prescribed herein if certificate of current immunization cannot be produced, and in addition, pay for the board of the animal for which it was impounded. The amount paid for the board of the dog or cat shall accrue to the credit of the city or county, depending upon the jurisdiction of the pound in which the animal was confined. At his direction, the said impounding officer may sell any dog or cat not redeemed or claimed or otherwise disposed of, to any purchaser desiring the said animal, which said purchaser must comply with all the provisions of the chapter."

The owner is given notice that his pet had no rabies tag. If the owner fails to pay for immunization, the pet may be given away or put to sleep. Dogs impounded for lack of a tag signifying rabies vaccination may be humanely disposed of if not claimed within seven days of "due notice to the owner."

> In order to redeem a pet, the owner must pay for the immunization, the costs of impoundment, plus a penalty, if he cannot produce the certificate of immunization. The impoundment officer may sell the pet to any purchaser if it is not claimed. If not purchased, the pet will be destroyed after a specified period of time (ordinarily thirty days).

> Lost tags, dogs immunized in another state or country, or difficulty in finding the owner have led to a host of hot-blooded cases. Usually, the government wins.

2-7. Quarantine of animals

The following sections are included to show what sort of explanatory text is furnished to pet owners regarding quarantine.

> "(a) Whenever the rabies officer or the health officer shall receive information that a human being has been bitten or exposed by a dog or cat required to be immunized against rabies, the health officer or his authorized agent shall cause said dog or cat to be placed in quarantine under the direct supervision of a duly licensed veterinarian for rabies observation as prescribed herein above. It shall be unlawful for any person having knowledge that a human being has been bitten or exposed by a dog or cat to fail to notify one or more of the aforementioned officers.

> (b) When said dog or cat is unowned, as determined by the rabies officer or the health officer after reasonable investigation, or where the owner of a dog or cat agrees in writing, or when ordered by the health officer, the animal shall be humanely destroyed immediately after the exposure and the

head shall be submitted for rabies examination to the State Health Department laboratory.

(c) The period of quarantine for animals other than domesticated dogs and cats which have bitten or exposed a human being shall be determined by the Department of Public Health upon consultation with the US Public Health Service. Provided, however, for those animal species where reliable epidemiological data are lacking regarding duration of rabies virus secretion from the salivary glands, said animals shall be humanely destroyed and the head submitted for rabies examination to the State Health Department.

(d) It shall be a violation of this chapter for the owner of such animal to refuse to comply with the lawful order of the health officer in any particular case. It is unlawful for the owner to sell, give away, transfer to another location or otherwise dispose of any such animal that is known to have bitten or exposed a human being until it is released from quarantine by the rabies officer, duly licensed veterinarian or by the appropriate health officer.

(e) Instructions for the quarantine of the offending animal shall be delivered in person or by telephone to the owner by the health officer or his authorized agent. If such instructions cannot be delivered in such manner, they shall be mailed by regular mail, postage prepaid and addressed to the owner of the animal. The affidavit or testimony of the health officer or his authorized agent, who delivers or mails such instructions, shall be prima facie evidence of the receipt of such instructions by the owner of the animal. Any expenses incurred in the quarantine of the offending animal under this section shall be borne by the owner. [Cases abound surrounding the adequacy of notice attempted or conveyed to the owner].

(f) The veterinarian under whose care the offending animal has been committed for quarantine shall promptly report the results of his observation of said animal to the attending physician of the human being bitten or exposed and the appropriate health officer.

(g) Canine corps dogs and seeing eye dogs shall be exempt from the quarantine period where such exposure occurs in the line of duty and evidence of proper immunization against rabies is presented, but shall be examined immediately at the end of 10 days by a licensed veterinarian, who shall report the results of his examination to the appropriate health officer as previously authorized."

2-8. Animals exposed to rabid animal.

"Those domesticated species, for which anti-rabies vaccine is recognized and recommended, upon exposure or potential exposure to a known rabid animal, shall be humanely destroyed or slaughtered immediately. Provided, however, the owner may have the option of quarantining said animals based on the recommendations of the Department of Public Health upon consultation with the US Public Health Service.

Every domesticated animal for whom an anti-rabies vaccination exists, shall be immediately slaughtered or destroyed. However, at the option of the owner, the animal may be quarantined as provided by the US Department of Public Health.

Each county, annually, shall select a qualified veterinarian as rabies control officer."

2-9. Impoundment, etc., of animals running at large on streets, etc.

"All cities and towns of this state shall have the power to regulate and prevent the running at large on the streets of all horses, mules, cows, hogs, dogs or other animals and to pass all laws necessary for the impounding and sale of such animals and destruction of dogs and to regulate and prohibit the driving of livestock in droves through the streets of a city or town."

> In Pamplona, Spain, this law would be unpopular. Clever Spaniards would likely circumvent the statute by disguising the bulls as shoppers mobbing the after-Thanksgiving sale. I would expect that if this guise were employed, the number of tramplings and gorings would be far short of the carnage produced by the real after-Thanksgiving sale.

2-10. Animal Research Facilities.

"The Legislature has found and determined that there have been an increasing number of illegal acts committed against animal research and production facilities involving injury to humans or animals, criminal trespass, and damage to property. These acts not only abridge the property rights of the owner of the facility, they also damage the public interest by jeopardizing crucial scientific, biomedical, or agricultural research or production. These actions can also threaten the public safety by exposing communities to serious public health concerns and may substantially disrupt or damage research.

Therefore, it is in the interest of the people of the State to protect the welfare of humans and animals as well as productive use of public funds to prohibit unauthorized possession, alteration, or destruction of agricultural, educational, or research records, equipment, and animals."

> This is a stark example of a state moving in reverse. In short, the law protects no animals from being tortured, destroyed, or injured in the course of animal research. The law protects the laboratory, facility, or entity from having the animals rescued, while anyone trying to rescue such animals is penalized. A similar example of animal-unfriendly legislation is Alabama's law stating that "It shall be unlawful for any person fishing in the waters of

> Alabama, upon catching a Garfish, to release it, live, back into the waters of Alabama." Sturgeons and garfish look a lot alike, and sturgeons are now endangered in Alabama. I wonder why?

2-11. Housing accommodations for the blind with dog.

"Every totally or partially blind person who has a guide dog or who obtains a guide dog shall be entitled to full and equal access to all housing accommodations provided for in this section, and he shall not be required to pay extra compensation for such guide dog, but shall be liable for any damage done to the premises by such guide dog."

> This is one of those genuinely humanitarian laws in that it gives blind persons and their guide dogs the absolute right to housing—at no extra charge. This provision is usually applied in the lease of a house, apartment, motel, or hotel room to the unsighted person and his or her dog.

> Other laws give unfettered rights to the blind in hotels, restaurants, public conveyances, and the like regarding the admission of their faithful guide.

> If you should see an unsighted person in a movie theater, his seat (beside his dog, bless his heart) would invariably be behind someone wearing a huge hat.

2-12. Dog Guides.

"No owner, lessee, proprietor, manager, superintendent, agent or employee of any place of public accommodation, amusement or recreation, including, but not limited to, any inn, hotel, restaurant, eating establishment, barbershop, billiard parlor, store, public conveyance, theater, motion-picture house, public educational institution or elevator shall refuse to permit a dog guide to accompany a blind person who is being led by the dog guide; provided further, that such blind person shall present for inspection credentials issued by an accredited school for training dog guides. Any person who violates this section shall be guilty of a misdemeanor and, upon conviction shall be fined an amount not to exceed $50.00."

> This is a most necessary statute that prohibits interfering with a blind person and his or her seeing-eye dog entering and remaining in any public place. The law says, however, that the blind person may be asked to produce credentials from an accredited school for seeing-eye dogs. Finally, the dog must be in a harness. Some states, in response to counterfeits, have been forced to pass laws making it a crime for a sighted person to put his dog in a harness and pass himself off as an unsighted person soliciting charity.

2-13. Definitions Related to Practice of Veterinary Medicine

"For the purposes of this article, the following terms shall have the following meanings ascribed by this section:

(1) ACCREDITED SCHOOL OF VETERINARY MEDICINE. Any veterinary college or division of a university or college that offers the degree of doctor of veterinary medicine or its equivalent and is accredited by the American Veterinary Medical Association (AVMA).

(2) ANIMAL. Any animal or mammal other than man, including birds, fish, reptiles, wild or domestic, living or dead.

(3) APPLICANT. A person who files an application to be licensed to practice veterinary medicine or licensed as a veterinary technician.

(4) BOARD. State Board of Veterinary Medical Examiners.

(5) CONSULTING VETERINARIAN. A veterinarian licensed in another state who gives advice or demonstrates techniques to a licensed veterinarian or group of licensed state

veterinarians. A consulting veterinarian shall not utilize this privilege to circumvent the law.

(6) DIRECT SUPERVISION. The veterinarian is on the premises and is quickly and easily available and the animal has been initially examined by a veterinarian and examined by a veterinarian at such other times as acceptable veterinary medical practice requires, consistent with the particular delegated animal health care task.

(7) EMERGENCY. The animal has been placed in a life threatening condition and immediate treatment is necessary to sustain life.

(8) PRACTICE OF VETERINARY MEDICINE. To diagnose, treat, correct, change, relieve, or prevent animal disease, deformity, defect, injury, or other physician or mental condition; including the prescription or administration of any drug, medicine, biologic, apparatus, application, anesthesia, or other therapeutic or diagnostic substance or technique on any animal including but not limited to acupuncture, dentistry, animal psychology, animal chiropractic, dentistry, animal psychology, animal chiropractic, theriogenology, surgery, including cosmetic surgery, any manual, mechanical, biological, or chemical procedure for testing for pregnancy or for coffecting sterility or infertility or to render service or recommendations with regard to any of the above."

> The State Veterinary Practice Act sets out very stringent standards for those persons committed to caring for animals. A licensed veterinarian must have graduated from a school accredited by the American Veterinary Medical Association.

"Animal is defined under the Act as any mammal other than man, including birds, fish, reptiles, living or dead, wild or domestic.

Among other things directed to the correction, treatment, prevention and diagnosis of defect, deformity or disease, veterinarians may use acupuncture, dentistry, animal psychology, animal chiropractic, theriogenology, surgery, cosmetic surgery, tests for sterility and tests for infertility."

> This law provides for a broad range of treatments, cures and preventative measures. Animal psychology, a source of mirth to some, is sometimes necessary and often indispensable. As I learned from my two veterinarian uncles, don't every pick the shy, elusive, cowering pup from a litter. Such a pet will often grow up to be of an unpredictable disposition—aggressive and ferocious at certain times, docile and cowardly at others.

> Under this act, the practice of veterinary medicine also provides for that of a veterinary intern (one working toward a ECFVG Certificate and supervised by a licensed veterinarian).

> A Veterinary Student Preceptee is one attending an accredited veterinary school which has an accepted extern or preceptor program.

> The law also provides for veterinary technicians, licensed veterinary assistants, veterinary technologists, animal technologists, and animal technicians. Such positions require a post-high school course accredited by the AVMA Committee.

2-14. "Grandfather clause".

"Any person holding a valid license to practice veterinary medicine in the state on or before [a specified date], shall be recognized as a licensed veterinarian and shall be entitled to retain this status so long as he or she complies with this article and the administrative code of the board."

2-15. Abandoned animals.

"Any animal placed in the custody of a licensed veterinarian for the treatment, boarding, or other care which shall be unclaimed by its owner or his or her agent for a period of more than 10 days after written notice by registered or certified mail, return receipt requested, to the owner or his or her agent at his or her last known address shall be deemed to be abandoned and may be turned over to the nearest Humane Society or dog, pound or sold to collect the lien pursuant to previous sections."

2-16. "Good Samaritan act;" emergency care.

"(a) Any licensed veterinarian who in good faith as a volunteer and without fee renders emergency care or treatment to a domestic animal shall not be liable in a suit for damages as a result of his or her acts or omissions which may occur during emergency care or treatment, nor shall be or she be liable to any animal hospital for its expense if under emergency conditions he or she orders an animal hospitalized or causes his or her admission to a hospital.

(b) Any licensed veterinarian who in good faith renders or attempts to render emergency care at the scene of an accident or emergency to the human victim or victims thereof shall not be liable for any civil damages as a result of any act or omissions by persons rendering or attempting to render the emergency care."

> The reader may be disappointed to learn that I have chosen to omit from this volume my contemplated chapter on *Neuropsychology and the Iguana*. The correspondence school reported that my tuition payment had been declined by Master Card and no degree would be forthcoming. They also requested that I return both pages of the course material and text.

2-17. Tampering with racing animals prohibited.

"No person shall influence or have any understanding or connivance with (1) any owner, trainer, jockey, driver, groom or other person associated with or arrested in any stable, horse or race in which any horse participates, or any owner, trainer, handler, groom or other person associated with or interested in any kennel, greyhound or race in which any greyhound participates, to prearrange or predetermine the results of any horse race or greyhound race, nor shall any person stimulate or depress a horse or greyhound, for the purpose of affecting the results of a race, by use of any electrical device or any electrical equipment or by any mechanical or other device not generally accepted as regulation racing equipment, nor shall any person stimulate or depress a horse or greyhound through the administration of any drug or chemical, or knowingly enter any horse or greyhound in any race within a period of 24 hours after any drug or chemical has been administered to such horse or greyhound, for the purpose of increasing or retarding the speed of such horse or greyhound.

No person shall, except for medical purposes, administer any poison, drug, medicine or other substance to any horse or greyhound entered or about to be entered in any race, or expose such substance to a horse or greyhound with the intent that it be taken, or cause any foreign substance to be taken by or placed upon or in the body of such horse or greyhound, with intent to impede or increase its speed endurance, health or physical or mental condition.

Any person violating the provisions of this section shall be guilty of a felony and upon conviction thereof, shall be imprisoned for not less than one year or more than 10 years, or fined not less than $5,000.00 nor more than $10,000.00 or both, in the discretion of the court."

> Isn't it rather strange that almost every other law dealing with animals is a misdemeanor, yet this is a felony—in states that disallowed almost all forms of gambling for years and years?

> Could this mean the huge investments by gamblers into thoroughbreds and racing caused the animal's intrinsic value to soar? No, I suspect it is simply the voice of big money speaking into the ear of the legislature.

2-18. Theft of property in the second degree.

"(a) The theft of property which exceeds $250.00 in value but does not exceed $1,000.00 in value, and which is not taken from the person of another, constitutes theft of property in the second degree.

(b) The theft of any livestock which includes cattle, swine, horses, mules, asses, or sheep, regardless of their value, constitutes theft of property in the second degree."

> This code section states that the theft of any animal (although "livestock" is the term used) amounts to theft in the second degree. This is a good law for pet owners. One likes to think he enjoys a range of protection—from theft to the injury or death of an animal—if one owns and loves a pet.

2-19. Anti Obscenity Enforcement Act.

"Sexual Conduct—Any act of sexual intercourse, masturbation, urination, defecation, lewd exhibition of the genitals, sado-masochistic abuse, bestiality or the fondling of sex organs of animals; any other physical contact with a person's unclothed genitals, public area, buttocks or the breast or breasts of a female, whether alone or between members of the same sex or opposite sex or between a human and an animal in acts of sexual stimulation, gratification or perversion."

> No comment.

2-20. Illegal to Use Animals in Certain Acts.

States have been vigilant in passing legislation prohibiting the twisted exhibition of dog fighting. As far as other amusements or displays that brutally involve animals, most states use the application of a general statute forbidding cruelty to prohibit the sort of spectacles we've all seen at fairs or exhibitions. When the owner of a cruel act opposes the statute in court as vague or inapplicable, a municipality will often pass a specific ordinance to prohibit the exhibition of cruelty.

Some six or seven years ago, at a State Fair, an operator announced an exhibition of "Diving Mules." (Said mules would take a one-hundred-foot drop into a five-foot deep tank.) Since he had not been stopped in other states, he sued to overcome public objection. The city that hosted the fair quickly passed an ordinance prohibiting diving mules.

Diving mules, chimpanzees racing motorcycles, and similar inhumane manipulations are now targeted by states and municipalities. Bear wrestling, an exhibition that has been around for years, is specifically prohibited by many states as noted in the following statute.

2-21. Bear Wrestling.

"(a) A person commits the offense of unlawful bear exploitation if he or she knowingly does any one of the following:

(1) Promotes, engages in, or is employed at a bear wrestling match,

(2) Receives money for the admission of another person to a place kept for bear wrestling.

(3) Sells, purchases, possesses, or trains a bear for bear wrestling.

(4) For purposes of exploitation, subjects a bear to surgical alteration in any form, including, but not limited to, declawing, tooth removal, and severing tendons.

(b) unlawful bear exploitation is a Class B felony and is punishable as provided by law."

> How would a woman feel if she were passed over for the title of Miss America due to an old conviction for bear exploitation?

> Any aspect of bear wrestling, promotion, etc., is punishable as a Class B felony. One could do ten years for this. This is particularly unfair if the bear gets off—and the bear started the fight.

Other inhumane exhibitions are prohibited by more broad-spectrum legislation.

"Willfully and maliciously killing or injuring animals; administering poison to animals, punishment, costs of animal care; probation, need for counseling, relinquishment of animals; exceptions:

(1) As used in this section, 'animal' means any vertebrate other than a human being.

(2) A person who willfully, maliciously and without just cause or excuse kills, tortures, mutilates, or causes to be injured, any animal as defined herein."

"Cruelty to animals.

(1) A person is guilty of cruelty to animals if the person intentionally, knowingly, recklessly, or with criminal negligence:

(2) Knowingly compromises the safety of the animal, cruelly abuses the animal, tortures or otherwise needlessly endangers the animal.

(3) A person is guilty of aggravated cruelty to an animal if the person:

(a) Tortures an animal;

(b) administers poison or poisonous substances to an animal without having to do so.

(c) kills or causes to be killed an animal without having a legal privilege to do so.

(4) A violation of Subsection (3) is:

(a) a class A misdemeanor is committed intentionally or knowingly;

(b) a class B misdemeanor if committed recklessly; and

(c) a class C misdemeanor is committed with criminal negligence.

(5) It is a defense to prosecution under this section that the conduct of the actor towards the animal was:

(a) by a licensed veterinarian using accepted veterinary practice."

2-22. Turtle Sales and Possession to be Strictly Regulated; Salmonella.

All states have statutes concerning turtles and the prevalence of salmonella, which may be contracted from handling them. Louisiana's law probably represents the most comprehensive example of this legislation. The regulation applies under public health laws as well as those applicable to pet shops.

"Regulation of sale of turtles:

(a) As used in this section, 'turtle' means any reptile means any reptile commonly known as turtles, tortoises or terrapins but shall not include a turtle used solely for agricultural, scientific or educational purposes.

(b) No turtle with a carapace length of less that four inches or with viable turtle eggs may be sold in this state.

(c) No person may sell a live turtle with a carapace length of four inches or greater unless (1) a caution notice is posted by the person selling turtles which warns that the transmission of salmonella disease by turtles is possible: (2) at the time of the sale of the turtle, the seller furnishes the buyer with a copy of the caution notice and information obtained from a veterinarian regarding the proper care and feeding for the species of turtle which is being sold; (3) the buyer signs a form stating that he has read the notice provided if the buyer is less than sixteen years of age, such form shall be signed by a parent or guardian; (4) the turtle is not a species identified by the Commissioner of Environmental Protection as endangered, threatened or of special concern in regulations adopted under section 26-306; and (5) the seller receives, and retains on file for inspection by the Commissioner of Agriculture, written verification that such turtle was bred at a licensed commercial fish farm or commercial aquaculture facility and was not collected from the wild.

(d) Any person who violates any provision of this section or section 19a-102b shall be fined not more than one hundred dollars. The Commissioner of Agriculture may suspend the pet shop license of any pet shop, as defined in section 22-327, which violates any provision of this section or section 19a-102b.

(e) On or before October 1, 1996, the Commissioner of Public Health shall evaluate the public health effect of the sale of turtles in this state and shall submit a report of his findings to the General Assembly.

(f) The Commissioner of Public Health may adopt regulations, in accordance with the provisions of chapter 54, to carry out the provisions of this section."

> Permit me to ask a question of any readers who are, say, thirty-five years of age or older. Do you not vividly recall family trips to Florida or some other holiday venue, where little turtles were sold for twenty-five to fifty cents? Invariably the little creatures had their shells brightly painted with a likeness of the state of the seller. As kids, we loved and kissed on these half-dollar sized pets and gave them names or nicknames. Later, we'd be torn apart as our parents would say, "No, you can't take Tillie home. He'd only get lost like the chameleon did and we'd have to call the fumigator back."

> Did our parents know about salmonella? Either way, the discovery of salmonella on and around turtles has incited a gaggle of laws and restrictions.

Chapter Three

Dogs and Cats:

Laws Protecting Dogs and Cats, Laws Protecting Their Owners, Laws Obligating the Owners, and Laws Protecting Third Parties

"My sheep wandered through all the mountains, and upon every high hill: yea, my flock was scattered upon all the face of the earth, and none did search or seek after them."

Ezekiel 34:6

3-1. Dogs and Cats to be Confined to Premises (Where County or City has Adopted this Provision).

"(a) Every person owning or having in charge any dog or cat shall at times confine such dog or cat to the limits of his own premises or the premises on which such dog or cat are regularly kept. Nothing in this section shall prevent the owner of any dog or cat or other person or persons having a dog or cat in his or their charge from allowing such dog or cat to accompany such owner or other person or persons elsewhere than on the premises on which such dog or cat is or are regularly kept. Any person violating this section shall be guilty of a misdemeanor and shall be fined.

(b) This section shall not apply to the running at large of any dog within the corporate limits of any city or town in this state that requires a license tag to be kept on dogs and cats nor shall this section apply in any county in this state until the same has been adopted by the county commission of such county."

> If a county has not adopted this provision of the state law, dogs with rabies tags may run free. This is usually the case in sparsely populated counties.

> This law is a little vague in that it requires an owner to keep his dog on his own premises. However, the law does not state that the dog or cat must be kept in a fenced area, or that the owner even have a fence. This is a good law for dogs and cats who can read law. For those who can't, their owners can be liable for injury or damage caused by a dog or cat off his owner's premises.

> This law will be modified by local leash laws, which actually require the dog or cat be confined on a leash, in a fenced area, or on the owner's property. Such a law, of course, can lead to a situation in which the dog or cat, in its owner's confinement, injures another. This law will be discussed in the next section. For our present purposes,

> the dog or the cat gets one free bite. That is to say that, unless or until it bites or attempts to bite a person, it is presumed under the law to be of a peaceful temperament. After that, his vicious propensities are "known" to the owner who may incur civil liability.

3-2. Leash Laws.

> Leash laws are almost exclusively passed by cities and townships. State legislators had, at times, enacted laws requiring pets be confined to premises, and only taken off premises under the control of the owner. Municipalities deemed that the word control was indefinite and inadequate. Thus, leash laws require a pet to be on a leash or harness or be subject to impoundment.

"The governing body of any city may adopt regulations or ordinances requiring that dogs within the confines of any such city be kept on a leash or otherwise restrained and may, by resolution directed to the circuit court of such city, request the court to order a referendum as to whether any such ordinance so adopted shall become effective in the city. Such referendum shall be held and adopted shall become effective in the city. Such referendum shall be held and conducted, and the results thereof ascertained and certified in accordance with Section 24.2-684. The court shall require the governing body to give appropriate notice of the time, place and subject matter of such referendum.

'Leash' means a cord, rope, strap, or chain which shall be securely fastened to the collar or harness of a dog or other animal and shall be of sufficient strength to keep such dog or other animal under control."

3-3. Pet Owner's Civil Liability for Injury, Damage or Death to Animals (Committed by Dog–Not Confined).

For purposes of clarity, this section is not meant to address civil liability for known vicious or dangerous animals, which will be discussed in section 3-7. This statute defines a situation in which a dog who has a peaceful temperament goes off its owner's premises and inflicts injury. The dog's owner may then be sued.

"If any dog, not being at the time on the premises of the owner or person having charge thereof, shall kill or injure any livestock or other domestic animal, dog or cat, the owner or person having such dog in charge shall be liable for damages sustained by the killing or maiming of any livestock or animal and for the full costs of the action."

> Incidentally, the word "maim" is derived from the Middle English word *maimen—the practice of knocking out teeth, gouging out eyes, or breaking the nose in order to render a warrior less able to fight.*

> This law says that a dog not on the premises of its owner makes the owner liable for the injury to, or killing of, any livestock. What is not addressed is the liability of an owner if some livestock wanders on the premises of the dog's owner. Obviously, if Fido has been prudent, he will not yet have used up his free bite.

"No person shall keep any dog which has been known to kill or worry sheep or other stock without being set upon the same. Any person knowingly keeping such dog is liable for double the value of all stock killed or injured by such dog, such damages to be recovered by the owner of such stock before any court of competent jurisdiction and no action shall be maintained against anyone for killing such dog."

> True, a worrisome dog must not be allowed to set upon sheep or any other animals. Worrisome or incessant barking, as well as threatened or actual attacks, may cause an animal to become spooked, unruly, or even die of fright. Let me emphasize, however, that the penalty is extreme; not only is the owner civilly liable, but his or her animals may be killed—legally.

> I had a border collie whose inborn characteristics and behavior caused it to try to herd my horses. Horses don't herd. So the dog nipped and barked, circled and dodged, tirelessly trying to herd the poor Arabians. That sort of behavior should not be allowed.

> That border collie now resides on a cattle ranch where it is an indispensable farm hand. It still barks at the livestock, but its genetically-engineered herding instinct is an asset to the rancher. The fact that the ranch occupies two hundred acres within a wilderness area make it unlikely that anyone, save the cattle, will be unduly disturbed.

3-4. Pet Owner's Civil Liability to Guests, Licenses, Permittees; Trespassers; Persons on Owner's Property; Lawful Presence; Committed by Pet Confined.

Simply, in the following case, the dog's bite occurs on its owner's premises:

"If any dog or cat shall, without provocation, bite or injure any person who is at the time at a place where he or she has a legal right to be, the owner of such dog or cat shall be liable in damages to the person so bitten or injured, but such liability shall arise only when the person so bitten or injured is upon property owned or controlled by the owner of such dog or cat at the time such bite or injury occurs or when such person has been immediately prior to such time on such property and has been pursued therefrom by such dog or cat."

Here is an important law to take note of, especially if your pet's temperament is a little unpredictable.

This section states that if a dog or cat bites or injures any person, without provocation, and that person was in a place where he or she had a right to be, the owner is liable for damages. However, this bite must occur on the premises of the pet owner, or as the victim was being pursued from said premises. The law classifies persons as guests (invitees), licensees (permittees), or trespassers. A guest is on the premises by invitation. A licensee is there under a right. These classes are protected. A trespasser—for instance, a thief—is trespassing and does not enjoy the law's protection, except that he may not be trapped or intentionally harmed.

For, say, a faithful bulldog named Alphonse, a nip occurring on the premises is a strike; a nip occurring on the sidewalk is a spare. Recall, however, the usual common law defense of the free bite. Thereafter, the law will presume the owner knew or had reason to be aware of the dog's propensity to bite.

3-4a. Specific classes of persons lawfully on owner's property in order to carry out duty.

"For the purpose of this chapter a person shall be considered to be lawfully upon the private property of the owner of such pet when he is on such property in the performance of any duty imposed upon him by the laws of this state or by the laws of the United States or the postal laws and regulations of the United States, when reading meters, when delivering milk, when making repairs to any public utility or service upon said premises or when on such property upon the invitation, wither expressed or implied of the owner or lessee of such property."

This refers to licensees (permittees) as are described above. The law also presumes an owner to know that his guest, an invitee, is entitled to be protected from the bite of a dog who has never before shown a predisposition to bite.

The law sets out the classes of persons who are legally entitled to be considered rightfully on the owner's premises. They are then qualified for the right, if bitten, to file a civil action for damages. Those classes include mailmen, meter readers, telephone company men, power company men, FBI agents, policemen, sheriffs, and under some statutes—believe it or not—agents of the Atomic Energy Commission.

One, however, should not presume that Fido will be predisposed to admire and respect the agents. On the contrary, it may be prudent to keep Fido restrained while entertaining said agents. In fact, no case exists of an AEC agent having been bitten. In my opinion, I believe that lawmakers must have been partaking of a wine tasting when they included these individuals. If not, then there is no legitimate excuse for including such a preposterous proposition.

3-4b. Nuisance.

An owner or keeper of an animal should understand, however, that even if his or her pet or other animal is kept securely on the owner's premises, the owner may still be liable to another person under the theory of nuisance.

The old but authoritative legal definition of nuisance is "anything that works hurt, inconvenience or damage to another. The inconvenience complained of must not be fanciful or such as would affect only one fastidious taste, but it should be such as would affect an ordinary reasonable man."

> Put plainly, Fido's adorable "singing" may be regarded as "incessant and odious barking" by a neighbor. Such is a private nuisance, for which the owner can be sued. Additionally, there is the criminal offense known as nuisance or public nuisance. In this case, the general public (i.e., a neighborhood) may be held to be the victim of a pervasive stench or a terrible racket. Such an action may be brought by the prosecutor or attorney general.

3-5. Defenses Available to the Owner of the Pet in Civil Actions

"The owner of such pet shall, however, be entitled to plead and prove in mitigation of damages that he had no knowledge of any circumstance indicating such pet to be or to have been vicious or dangerous or mischievous, and, it he does so, he shall be liable only to the extent of the actual expenses incurred by the person so bitten or injured as a result of the bite or injury."

> This section lists the defenses available to the owners of dogs or other pets that bite. The first defense is that the owner had no knowledge of any prior instance of the pet being vicious, dangerous, or mischievous. If the owner did have knowledge, then he or she is liable for actual and exemplary damages (exemplary damages can be awarded in addition to actual damages for behavior shown to be willful or malicious). This is, in effect, the codification of the common-law rule of the free bite.

> A second defense available to the owner is the case in which the injured party provoked the animal, thus bringing about the bite or attack.

> The third common defense is assumption of the risk. This can be exemplified by a sign posted on a panther's cage reading "DANGER—MAN EATING PANTHER—

KEEP OUT!" After reading said sign, an individual climbs into the cage to see if the sign is really true.

Killing dogs; dogs as nuisances

"(a) Legal to kill certain dogs—Any person may kill any dog which he sees in the act of pursuing or wounding or killing any domestic animal, wounding or killing other dogs, cat or household pets, or pursuing, wounding or attacking human beings, whether or not such a dog bears the license tag required by the provisions of this act. There shall be no liability on such persons in damages or otherwise for such killing.

(b) Private nuisance—Any dog that enters any field or enclosure where domestic animals are confined, provided that the enclosure is adequate for the purpose intended, shall constitute a private nuisance, and the owner or tenant of such field, or their agent or servant, may detain such dog and turn it over to the local police authority or state dog warden or employee of the department. While so detained, the dog shall be treated in a humane manner."

3-6. Pet Owners Criminal Liability for Causing or Allowing a Known Vicious or Dangerous Animal (Under His Control) to Injure or Destroy the Property, Persons or Pet of Another.

"By statute, in most states, and by legal implication in others, an owner may be criminally liable for intentionally causing or allowing a vicious or dangerous animal to injure or destroy the property, person or pet of another."

"Allowing Vicious Animal to Escape or Run at Large; Vicious Animal my be Killed; Liability of person Having Care or Custody of Animal Which Bothers, Injures or Kills Livestock of Another.

(1) Every person having the care or custody of any animal known to posses any vicious or dangerous tendencies, who allows it to escape or run at large in any place or manner liable to endanger the safety of any person, is guilty of a misdemeanor.

(2) Any person may lawfully and without liability for damages kill such an animal when reasonably necessary to protect his own safety or the public safety, or if the animal chases, worries, injures or kills his livestock on the land of any person other than that of the owner of the animal.

(3) Every person having the care or custody of an animal which chases, worries, injures or kills the livestock of another on land other than his own is liable to the owner of the livestock for damage to it.

(4) As used in this section, 'livestock' means all animals of the bovine, caprine, equine, ovine and porcine species, and all domesticated fowl and rabbits.

When any person owns or keeps a vicious animal of any kind and, as a result of his careless management of the same or his allowing the same to go at liberty, and another person, without fault on his part, is injured thereby, such owner or keeper shall be liable in damages for such 'injury.'"

> This section provides that the owner of a vicious animal who fails to confine it is responsible for damages if another person is injured, providing that person (victim) is injured through no fault of his own. An animal classified as *ferae naturae*, (e.g., an ocelot or lion) is guilty unless somehow proven innocent. This is true in all states.

> Defenses available to the owner of a known vicious or dangerous animal are few. Essentially, it is a situation of strict liability, like escape from jail. If a prisoner is there one day and not there the next, escape is proven by the absence of the prisoner from jail. Similarly, the owner of a known vicious animal, under the law, assumes all risks of injury or loss when he or she takes possession of the animal.

3-7. Pet Owners' Civil Liability for Injury, Damage or Death to Pets, Persons or Property Caused by Known Vicious or Dangerous Animal.

"A person who owns or keeps a vicious or dangerous animal of any kind and who, by careless management or by allowing the animal to go at liberty, causes injury to another person who does not provoke the injury by his own act may be liable in damages to the person so injured. In proving vicious propensity, it shall be sufficient to show that the animal was required to be at heel or on a leash by an ordinance of a city, county, or consolidated government."

> There is, of course, assumption of the risk by the injured party. This is a defense that may be available to an owner. Every year, in the U.S., some hapless soul endeavors to take twenty yards off a journey and tiptoes through the maximum-security enclosure of a two-thousand pound horned Brahma bull. This is the epitome of the "low-hamburger diet," as the dearly departed will never have the opportunity to chow down on one last McDonald's.

Definitions;

"(A) As used in this section:

(1) (a) 'Dangerous dog' means a dog that, without provocation, and subject to division (A) (1) (b) of this section, has chased or approached in either a menacing fashion or an apparent attitude of attack, or has attempted to bite or otherwise endanger any person, while that dog is off the premises of its owner, keeper, or harborer and not under the reasonable control of its owner, keeper, harborer, or some other responsible person, or not physically restrained or confined in a locked pen which has a top, locked fenced yard, or other locked enclosure."

Texas's statute, for example, provides that if a dog makes an unprovoked attack or unprovoked act (reasonably causing one to believe the dog will attack) off premises, the dog may be declared vicious after a hearing.

Failure of owners to comply with a notice of hearing can result in the destruction of the dog. A finding that the dog is dangerous can require the animal to be licensed as a vicious dog or be euthanized. It might appear that the state of Texas, in applying the death penalty, does not discriminate between animals and people. Most states, however, have similar provisions.

3-8. Lawful Killing of a Dog or Other Animal for its Injurious Acts.

In addition to statutes which provide for liability against owners of dangerous animals, including the loss of the animal's right to live, states typically have statutes allowing the killing of a pet, animal, or wolf-hybrid that assaults a person, or if it is necessary to stop an actual attack on a person or domestic animal. The killing provision is included in a single-purpose statute. That is, the statute doesn't address the liability of the owner of a vicious animal, only the legal rights to kill the animal.

One can readily see that this license to kill an animal when it becomes necessary to stop an attack is fraught with volatility. For example, a neighbor, just waiting for the chance, might see the allegedly vicious dog barking at a calf. "Ba-room" goes the shotgun. "A vicious life-threatening attack," he will say, "was prevented."

Or, say that an animal attacks or fights with another animal. The animals leave off the fight and the one chosen to be called vicious runs away. "Ba-room." A vicious attack was prevented by the owner of the dog not fired upon. Witnesses are not too plentiful on the back sides of hills and vales on private farmland.

Vicious Dog Control.

"(1) The county governing body may regulate, restrain, control, kill, or quarantine any vicious dog, whether such dog is licensed or unlicensed, by the adoption of an ordinance which substantially complies with the provisions of 7-5-103 through 7-5-107.

(2) A violation of any ordinance established as provided in subsection (1) is a misdemeanor."

Killing dogs; dogs as nuisances

"(a) Legal to kill certain dogs.—Any person may kill any dog which he sees in the act of pursuing or wounding or killing any domestic animal, wounding or killing other dogs, cat or household pets, or pursuing, wounding or attacking human beings, whether or not such a dog bears the license tag required by the provisions of this act. There shall be no liability on such persons in damages or otherwise for such killing.

(b) Private nuisance.—Any dog that enters any field or enclosure where domestic animals are confined, provided that the enclosure is adequate for the purpose intended, shall constitute a private nuisance, and the owner or tenant of such field, or their agent or servant, may detain such dog and turn it over to the local police authority or State dog warden or employee of the department. While so detained, the dog shall be treated in a humane manner.

(c) Licensed dogs not included.—Licensed dogs, when accompanied by their owner or handler, shall not be included under the provisions of this section unless caught in the act of pursuing, wounding or killing any domestic animal, wounding or killing any dogs, cats or household pets, or pursuing, wounding or attacking human beings."

Right to Kill Domestic Pets or Wolf-Hybrids Generally

"(A) A person may kill a domestic pet or wolf-hybrid that suddenly assaults him or her or when necessary to discontinue an attack upon the person or another person provided that the attack or assault does not occur while the domestic pet or wolf-hybrid if restrained, within an enclosure containing the domestic pet or wolf-hybrid, or on the premises of the owner.

(B) A domestic pet or wolf-hybrid found wounding, killing or worrying another domestic pet or wolf-hybrid, a domestic animal or fowl may be killed when the attendant circumstances are such that the killing is reasonably necessary to prevent injury to the animal or fowl which is the subject of the attack."

3-9. Rabid Pets, Owner's Liability.

"The owner or person in charge of any dog or cat, who knows that such dog or cat has been bitten by a rabid animal, or has knowledge of such facts that if followed up would disclose the facts that such dog or cat has been bitten by or exposed to a rabid animal, if such dog or cat becomes rabid and bites any person, stock, hogs or cattle, shall be liable to twice the damages sustained by the person injured, including appropriate medical treatment, such damages to be recovered in any court of competent jurisdiction (one having jurisdiction over the parties and the monetary limit to enforce its judgment)."

> This law places liability on the owner of a dog or cat bitten by a rabid animal (or, if the owner inquired, would

> or should know his dog or cat had been bitten by a rabid animal). Anyone who has seen the film *I Was a Teen-Age Werewolf* (starring a very young Michael Landon) will have a far superior understanding of rabid animals and the need for such a statute as this.

> In such cases, the owner is liable for twice the amount of damages, plus medical bills, if his now-rabid pet bites a person, another pet, a cow, or a pig. Raccoons should have been added, as these ever-present masked marauders seem to have a penchant not only for being prime carriers of rabies, but also for biting their animal friends.

Killing of Vicious or Mad Dog Authorized

"Any person may lawfully kill any vicious or mad dog running at large."

3-10. Prevention of Cruelty to Animals; Agencies and Enforcement Officers.

"The county commissions of the respective counties of this state may employ a suitable person or persons who shall be charged specially with the duty of enforcing all laws for the prevention of cruelty to animals, and to fix the compensation of such officer or officers, which shall be paid in the same manner as other salaries of county employees are paid, and such officer or officers, upon taking the oath as required to be taken by deputy sheriffs; shall be vested with all powers now vested by law in deputy sheriffs."

> County cruelty prevention officers are given the same powers as sheriffs to the extent that they may prosecute persons who have abused animals. The only problem consistent nationwide is that states budget too little money for this protection, and there are too few officers commissioned.

3-11. Neglected or Abused Animals; Care and Keeping by Humane Authority.

"Any duly authorized officer or employee of a recognized humane society shall have the right to take charge of any animal which is sick or disabled due to neglect or is being cruelly treated or abused and to provide care for such animal until it is deemed to be in suitable condition to be returned to its owner or to the person from whose custody such animal was taken.

The officer so taking such animal shall at the time of taking the animal give written notice to the owner or person from whose custody it was taken.

The necessary expenses incurred for the care and keeping of the animal after such notice by the humane society shall be a lien thereon and, if the animal is not reclaimed within 10 days from the giving of such notice, the humane society may spay or neuter then sell the animal to satisfy such lien. If the humane society determines that the animal cannot be sold, it may cause the animal to be otherwise disposed of."

> Such a law on the rights of a humane society or animal shelter is fair and equitable. It states that the society may take in an animal that is sick, injured, neglected, or appears to have been cruelly mistreated. The society must give the owner ten days notice of the taking in. The owner has ten days (from the date the notice is sent) to retrieve the pet and pay the reasonable costs of care and treatment.

> The problem here is that the owner who neglected or abused the animal can get it back upon paying roughly forty dollars to have it spayed or neutered. Then, theoretically, such a slob would likely feel he "double owns" the animal and may continue to have his way with it.

3-12. Destruction of Abandoned Animals.

"Any agent, officer or member of a duly incorporated society for the prevention and cruelty to animals may lawfully destroy or cause to be destroyed any animal found abandoned and not properly cared for which may appear, in the judgment of two reputable citizens called by him to view the same in his presence, to be superannuated, infirm, glandered, injured or diseased past recovery for any useful purpose."

> If a humane society or other society for prevention of cruelty to animals should find an old, feeble animal, or one that is sick or injured beyond recovery, upon the concurrence of any two persons the animal may be put to sleep. This presumes the animal is abandoned. The most distressing aspect of this law is the duty to find two reputable citizens. Since we obviously can't look among lawyers, politicians, or newspaper reporters, our search is limited.

> Chapter One discussed the euthanizing of animals and the methods allowed. There have been fights and lawsuits over the question of whether an animal was abandoned or not. A lost dog, without a collar, might well look abandoned to the humane society. A tragedy occurs if such an animal is put down when it's only hungry and lost. If no one claims the pet in ten days, the society tries to sell it and, failing that, will put the animal to sleep. Many societies will not put a pet out for adoption until an adopter is found, and then the animal is spayed or neutered before it is let out of custody.

> In practice, there have been nightmarish cases where a humane society has put an animal to sleep after being told by the owner "I'll be there in fifteen minutes!" This is extremely rare. However, in a case tried in my court in Birmingham, Alabama, an owner rushed in breathless

only to be told that his Grand Sire German Shepherd named Router should now be called Rowena, because he had been neutered.

Router's owner, a young African-American man, was a recently retired Army K-9 Corps handler. He had brought the dog home to Birmingham from Germany. Upon learning that his missing pet was at the pound, he called to say that Router was his pet as well as a champion, and he was en route to reclaim the dog. The owner seemed to be unable to persuade the person on the other end of the phone to hold off the neutering surgery for just ten minutes. Arriving at the pound, he discovered a slyly smiling director—and a neutered Grand Champion.

The Army veteran sued and recovered a modest sum in remuneration for the outrageous treatment visited upon himself and his pet. The Birmingham pound appealed and appealed the decision, however, "out of principle and precedent." It finally gave up the fight, leaving no true winner.

Methods of Destruction of Animals.

"(a) Required method—The required method of destruction shall be by the administration of an overdose of a barbiturate, barbiturate combinations, drug or drug combinations approved for this purpose by the Federal Drug Administration and in accordance with guidelines established by the Pennsylvania Department of Agriculture."

3-13. Cruelty to Animals—Criminal Penalties.

> This section is the chief vehicle for persons whose pet has been killed by an unruly teenager or a neighbor who takes the law into his or her own hands over such issues as the barking of a dog. The law sets out a fine of one thousand dollars and imprisonment for up to six months in the county jail on misdemeanor charges. Several states have passed legislation upgrading this to a felony when extreme cruelty or killing is involved, including Kansas, Kentucky, Arizona, Idaho, Illinois, Connecticut, and Alabama.

Criminal Penalties.

This particular law was enacted to prevent and punish various acts of cruelty to animals.

"A person commits the crime of cruelty to animals if, except as otherwise authorized by law, he intentionally or recklessly:

(1) Subjects any animal to cruel mistreatment; or

(2) Subjects any animal in his custody to cruel neglect; or

(3) Kills or injures without good cause any animal."

> This law (and similar ones across the nation) has saved countless animals from cruel or neglectful mistreatment when no other law allowed police to enter the premises of an abuser.

> Some ten to fifteen years ago, concerned people summoned police to a ramshackle house where the owner had kept—for years—two horses in an upstairs bedroom. When rescued, they were malformed and sick, but with care and treatment they were able to spend their last years in a lush pasture.

"(1) As used in this section, 'animal' means any vertebrate other than a human being.

(2) A person who willfully, maliciously and without just cause or excuse kills, tortures, mutilates, maims, or disfigures an animal or who willfully and maliciously and without just cause or excuse administers poison to an animal, or exposes an animal to any poisonous substance, other than a substance that is used for therapeutic veterinary medical purposes, with the intent that the substance be taken or swallowed by the animal, is guilty of a felony, punishable by imprisonment for not more than 4 years, or by a fine of not more than $5,000.00, or community service for not more than 500 hours or any combination of these penalties.

(3) As a part of the sentence for a violation subsection (2), the court may order the defendant to pay the costs of the prosecution and the costs of the care, housing, and veterinary medical care for the impacted animal victim, as applicable. If the court does not order a defendant to pay all of the applicable costs listed in this subsection, or orders only partial payment of these costs, the court shall state on the record the reasons for that action.

(4) If a term of probation is ordered for a violation of subsection (2), the court may order, as a condition of probation, that the defendant be evaluated to determine the need for psychiatric or psychological counseling, and, if determined appropriate by the court, to receive psychiatric or psychological counseling at his or her own expense.

(5) As a part of the sentence for a violation of subsection (2), the court may order the defendant not to own or possess an animal for any period of time determined by the court, which may include permanent relinquishment.

Torment, torture and cruelty: 'Torment, torture and cruelty' means every act, omission or neglect, whether by the owner or any other person, where unjustifiable physical pain, suffering or death is caused or permitted."

> Idaho and Illinois have statutes providing that, if vulgar ritual acts are performed and a child is forced to participate—by threat of death or injury to the child's pet—such acts constitute a felony. This type of statute is intended to protect children, but it protects their pets as well.

Ritualized abuse of a child.

"(a) A person is guilty of ritualized abuse of a child when he or she commits any of the following acts with, upon, or in the presence of a child as part of a ceremony, rite or any similar observance:

(1) actually or simulation, tortures, mutilates, or sacrifices any warm-blooded animal or human being;

(2) forces ingestion, injection or other application of any narcotic, drug, hallucinogen or anesthetic for the purpose of dulling sensitivity, cognition, recollection of, or resistance to any criminal activity;

(3) forces ingestion, or external application, of human or animal urine, feces, flesh, blood, bones, body secretions, non prescribed drugs or chemical compounds;

(4) involves the child in a mock, unauthorized or unlawful marriage ceremony with another person or representation of any force or deity, followed by sexual contact with the child;

(5) places a living child into a coffin or open grave containing a human corpse or remains;

(6) threatens death or serious harm to a child, his or her parents, family, pets, or friends."

3-14. Title to Pets.

Pets and animals are usually owned without benefit of title, as would be the case with legal ownership of land or a car. Pedigreed pets and registered animals entitle their owner to a certificate of registration, either from the breeder association, or, in the case of wild animals, the state.

Possession of an animal and proof of ownership are generally sufficient confirmation of custody, in lieu of title or registration. Proof could be a certificate of registration, a bill of sale, veterinary records, and the like. With rare exceptions, persons may not possess or own wild animals because their title is, by statute, vested in the state. Proof of ownership is essential for retrieval of a pet from a pound or animal welfare agency.

3-15. Dog Fighting.

"(a) It shall be a felony for any person:

(1) To own, possess, keep or train any dog with the intent that such dog shall be engaged in an exhibition of fighting with another dog;

(2) For amusement or gain, to cause any dog to fight with another dog, or cause any dogs to injure each other.

(3) To permit any act in violation of subdivisions (1) and (2) of this subsection.

(b) It shall be a felony for any person to be knowingly present, as a spectator, at any place, building, or tenement where preparations are being made for an exhibition of the fighting dogs, with the intent to be present at such preparations, or to be knowingly present at such exhibition or to knowingly aid or abet another in such exhibition [incidentally, "presence" presumes an intent to be there].

Any dog used to fight other dogs in violation of subsection (a) of this section, shall be confiscated as contraband by the sheriff or other law enforcement officers and shall not be returned to the owner, trainer or possessor of said dog. The court shall award the animals to the humane society or other agency handling stray animals. At its discretion, the humane society or other agency handling stray animals shall humanely dispatch or dispose of any confiscated dog.

(c) Any dog confiscated pursuant to subsection (b) of this section by the sheriff or other law enforcement officers shall be taken to the local humane society or other animal welfare agency.

(d) An appointed veterinarian or officer of the humane society or other animal welfare agency may upon delivery or at any time thereafter destroy the animal that is in his opinion injured, diseased, past recovery, or whose continued existence is inhumane and destruction is necessary to relieve pain or suffering.

(e) After confiscation, the humane society or other animal welfare agency may make application to the circuit court for a hearing to determine whether any animal seized pursuant to subsection (b) of this section shall be humanely destroyed due to disease, injury or lack of any useful purpose because of training or viciousness. The court shall set a hearing date not more than 30 days from the filing of the application and shall give notice of the same to the owners of the animals. Upon a finding by the court that the seized animals are diseased, injured or lacking any useful purpose due to training or viciousness, it shall be within the authority of the humane society or other animal welfare agency to humanely destroy such animal. Any animal found by the court not to be diseased, injured or lacking any useful purpose due to training or viciousness shall be delivered to a court-approved private veterinarian. Expenses incurred in connection with the housing, care or upkeep of the dogs by any person, firm, partnership, corporation or other entity shall be taxed against the owner.

(f) If any dog owner is convicted under subsection (a) of this section, the animal(s) shall be awarded to the local humane society or other animal welfare agency.

It shall be a felony to own, keep, posses or train any dog with the intent that the dog shall be engaged in an exhibition of fighting with another dog; for amusement or gain for one dog to fight with another dog.

It is also a felony to be a spectator at such an event.

Any dog within the above classification shall be taken into custody by a humane department.

Upon application to the circuit court, dogs irreparably injured shall be destroyed and those amenable to being restored will be placed in adoption programs, unless they are too vicious to be kept."

> For our purposes, a misdemeanor is a crime punishable by up to one year in the county jail. A felony is a crime punishable by a sentence of at least one year and one day, or longer, in the state prison. A lapsed parking meter is a misdemeanor; a robbery is a felony.

Chapter Four

Barnyard Animals

Horses, Cattle, Sheep, Pigs, Goats, Mules, and Chickens

"The horse was on his feet now…His hip bones stood out like an old cow's, his ribs showed like a washboard and his back was a mass of sores"

Gone With the Wind by Margaret Mitchell

4-1. Wanton or malicious injury, etc.; livestock.

"(a) Any person who unlawfully, wantonly or maliciously, kills, disables, disfigures, destroys, or injures the livestock of another while said livestock is on the premises of the owner of said livestock or on the premises of a person having charge thereof shall be guilty of a felony."

(b) In addition to being guilty of a felony, any person who unlawfully, wantonly or maliciously, kills, disables, disfigures, destroys, or injures the livestock of another while such livestock is on the premises of the owner of the livestock, or on the premises of a person having charge thereof shall be liable for damages sustained by the killing, disabling, disfiguring, or destroying of said livestock in an amount equal to double the value thereof.

(c) For purposes of this section, livestock is defined as horses, cows, swine, goats, sheep, mules, and assess."

> This section of the law, passed years and years ago in almost every state, makes it a felony to kill or injure an animal on its owner's property. At one time, this statute gave livestock more rights than a dog or cat because it imposed a felony punishment on the perpetrator of such actions. States have only recently bestowed such rights on dogs, cats, and other pets.

4-2. Wanton or malicious injury, etc., defenses.

"Upon the trial, the defendant may prove in mitigation or justification, as the jury may determine, that, at the time of the killing, disabling, disfiguring, destruction or injury, the animal killed, disabled disfigured, destroyed or injured was trespassing and had within six months previously thereto trespassed upon a growing crop, enclosed by a lawful fence or while such animal was running at large in violation of law. No conviction must be had, if it is shown that, before the commencement of the prosecution, compensation for the injury was made or tendered to the owner."

> This section of the law lists certain defenses to the malicious destruction of a horse, cow, or other animal that has broken into a fence (belonging to another person) that encloses growing crops. If the horse, cow, or other animal had broken into the fence enclosing the crops and it can be shown that the same animal had done the same thing within the previous six months, the crop owner may kill the animal in a wanton or malicious fashion. This also means that if a horse, cow, or other animal has broken into a garden fence, injuring vegetables or crops, the owner of the crop can kill the animal if he sees it running loose.

Allowing Vicious Animal to Escape or Run at Large; Vicious Animal May Be Killed; Liability of Person having Care or Custody of Animal Which Bothers, Injures or Kills Livestock of Another.

"(1) Every person having the care or custody of any animal known to possess any vicious or dangerous tendencies, who allows it to escape or run at large in any place or manner liable to endanger the safety or property of others has no right of recovery if the person killing the animal under proper circumstances pays the owner the reasonable cost of the animal."

> Furthermore, if the crop owner pays the animal's owner for having maliciously killed the animal, that payment constitutes a complete defense. This law, still good in Alabama and a handful of other states, comes from the age when cotton was king and all growing crops had the status of princes.

4-3. Rail fences; cattle, horses, mules.

"A rail fence five feet high, with the rails not more than 18 inches apart from the ground to the height of every three feet, shall be a lawful fence so far as cattle, horses and mules are concerned."

> Did you know that fences are required to be of a certain specified dimension in order to be legal? Consider this: in order to be allowed to bid on a wild mustang or other wild horse, the Department of the Interior requires one to prove that he has a ten-foot chain-link fence.

4-4. Barbed wire fences.

"A fence made of seven or more wires securely fastened to trees or posts not more than eight feet apart, the first four wires being of four-inch barb and not over four inches apart, commencing with the first four inches from the ground, the fifth wire not over six inches from the fourth, the sixth wire not over eight inches from the fifth and the seventh wire 15 inches from the sixth, shall be a lawful fence against all stock whatsoever."

> Barbed wire is, incidentally, a torture contraption for horses. A horse will kick and struggle to the death to free itself. Conversely, a cow will accept its entrapment and lie down until help comes.

4-5. Definitions.

"The term 'livestock' or 'animal,' where it occurs in this chapter, shall be held to be limited to and to refer to horses, mares, mules, jacks, jennies, colts, cows, calves, yearlings, bulls, oxen, sheep, goats, lambs, kids, hogs, shoats and pigs."

4-6. Running at large; generally.

"(a) It shall be unlawful for the owner of any livestock or animal, as defined herein above, to knowingly, voluntarily, negligently or willfully permit any such livestock or animal to go at large in this State either upon the premises of another or upon the public lands, highways, roads or streets of the State.

(b) Nothing in this section or elsewhere in this chapter shall be construed to make it unlawful for livestock or other animals to run at large on the premises of another when the owner or person in charge of the premises has consented in writing to let livestock or other animals run at large on the same or to subject the owner of such livestock or other animals to criminal prosecution therefore.

(c) There shall be no 'open range' counties in this state. This section shall apply to all counties within the state."

> This section of law makes it illegal for the owner of livestock to allow an animal to be estray (run at large). States are, however, divided regarding open range laws. The east, with more rainfall and population, places land at a premium. Owners of livestock are bound to abide by property lines and fences. The west, conversely, has millions of acres (much of it arid) and infrequent centers of population. Livestock owners require more acreage per animal in order to sustain growth. For this reason, fences have been scarce and animals allowed to roam and forage on the open range. Branding allows owners to keep track of their herds.

> The differences noted above set up a distinct liability situation. In the east, if a farm animal wanders across a road and is killed or kills a motorist, liability generally rests with the farmer if he willfully let the animal wander or

> knowingly placed it in an inadequate enclosure. In the west, however, if an animal crosses a road and is killed or kills a motorist, the farmer generally incurs no liability. There is only a slight possibility that the motorist will recover damages.

4-7. Owner's liability.

"(a) The owner of such livestock or animal being or running at large upon the premises of another or upon the public lands, roads, highways or streets in this [eastern] state shall be liable for all damages done to crops, shade or fruit trees or ornamental shrubs and flowers of any person, to be recovered before any court of competent jurisdiction; provided, that the owner of any stock or animal shall not be liable for any damages to any motor vehicle or any occupant thereof suffered, caused by or resulting from a collision with such stock or other animal, unless it be proven that such owner knowingly or willfully put or placed such stock upon such public highway, road or street where such damages were occasioned.

(b) The judgment of the court against the owner of such livestock or animal so depredating shall be a lien superior to all other liens on the livestock or animal causing the damage, except as to taxes."

> Thus, the owner of any animal that gets loose or otherwise runs at large is liable for any damage to crops, fruit trees, shade trees, ornamental shrubs, or flowers.

> If your automobile hits a cow on the highway in the east, the owner of the cow is liable if the cow was willfully let loose—because there are no range laws. Where range laws do exist, however, the driver of the automobile assumes the risk.

4-8. Immunity of those involved in equine activities.

"The legislature recognizes that persons who participate in equine activities may incur injuries as a result of the risks involved in those activities. The legislature also finds that the state and its citizens derive numerous economic and personal benefits from equine activities. The legislature finds, determines, and declares that for the immediate preservation of the public peace, health, and safety and to encourage equine activities, this legislation is to limit the civil liability of those involved in equine activities."

> This is a laughable example of a time-honored tradition—legislatures passing only those laws that some money-heavy private interest is willing to finance. So it is with this section. This law, passed to the pleasure of racing magnates, states that spectators, trainers, jockeys, and others who are injured in an activity related to horses may not bring suit against the at-fault party for injury or death. Surprisingly, this animal-related law is present in legal volumes throughout the country.

4-9. Use of sticks, whips, chains, etc., in livestock markets.

"Sticks, canes or whips shall not be used in such a manner so as to injure an animal. The use of chains, spikes, clubs or other injurious devices are hereby prohibited except under extreme circumstances where it is necessary to prevent injury to persons or other animals; and flappers, other noise making devices, electric prods of not more than six volts in strength and other contrivances which have been found to be equally effective shall be used wherever possible for such purposes."

> The use of chains, spikes, flappers or clubs is prohibited if used in a manner that will injure an animal. Like so very many statutes, however, an exception within the law causes it to have a limited effect. A comparable situation exists with conservation laws in southern states that

> allegedly protect beaches and marshes. State Environmental Agencies have been known to treat beachfronts and salt marshes like strip pits.

4-10. Sale or purchase by dealers of cattle, hogs, etc., after sunset or before sunrise.

"It shall be unlawful for any dealer to buy-or sell cattle, hogs, sheep or goats at any time after sunset or before sunrise."

> In trying to envision a state's motive for passing this law, consideration must be given to cattle rustling or theft by night. Beyond this, the legislators' motive would have to have been fear of vampires.

4-11. Estrays; generally.

"Any person who finds running at large about his residence or premises or the residence or premises of which he has charge any horse, more, mule, jack, jennet, cattle, hog, sheep or goat, the owner of which is unknown, may take up such animal as estray to be disposed of as provided in the sections herein above."

4-12. Notice of seizure—Lien for costs and damages.

"(a) Within five days after taking up an estray, notice of the seizure of such estray shall be furnished to the Department of Agriculture and Industries, accompanied by a complete description of the animal together with the time and place of seizure and the name and address of the seizure. The animal shall be described in such notice by kind, size, sex, markings, brands, color, stature and age.

(b) The seizor shall have a lien on the animal for the cost of keeping it and for the amount of any reasonable damages he may have suffered as a result of the animal being upon his premises.

Any person who finds running at large about his premises any horse, cow, mule, sheep or goat may take the animal in and will have a lien on it for costs of feeding. Thereafter, he may post notice with the Department of Agriculture and if not claimed, may sell the animal at auction."

> The proceeds are then divided, with the Department of Agriculture getting the lion's share.

4-13. Staking Livestock on Highway Right of Way.

"(a) It shall be unlawful for any person to stake, tie, hobble or pasture any animal of the cow kind, horse, mare, jack, mule, jennet or other equine animal, hog or animal of the swine kind, sheep or goat upon the right-of-way of any highway in this state.

(b) Any person having charge of or owning any such animal who knowingly permits such animal to be staked, tied, hobbled or pastured on the right-of-way of any highway in this state shall be guilty of a misdemeanor and shall be punished as provided by law for misdemeanors."

4-14. Enforcement.

"Every peace officer of this state is empowered to take up any such animal staked, tied, hobbled or pastured on any highway in this state in the same manner as is provided by law for the taking up of estrays or animals running at large."

> This is one you won't see happen on an episode of *Cops*. I have yet to see a State Trooper trying to get a mule into the back seat of a cruiser.

4-15. Admissibility of certificate of registration in civil actions or criminal proceedings as to title or right of possession.

"In all civil actions or in any criminal proceedings when the title or right of possession of livestock is involved, a copy of the certificate of livestock brand registration verified by affidavit of the commissioner shall be received in evidence by the court as evidence of the registration of such brand in accordance with the requirements of this article."

4-16. Furnishing, etc., of forms for registration, re-registration and transfer of brands by department.

"The department shall prescribe and furnish forms on which applications for registration, re-registration and transfer of livestock brands shall be made and shall furnish such forms to the sheriff and the county agricultural agent of each county of the state to be distributed on request to livestock owners desiring to make application for registration of brands and such applications may also be furnished to applicants by the department."

> Yes, cattle, sheep and horses can be legally branded in most states. Believe it or not, the law, by statute, recognizes a brand as legally admissible evidence in court. Branding is just as painful to the animals as it looks and sounds.

4-17. Dipping of horses, mules or asses kept in tick infested lots, ranges, etc.

"All horses, mules and asses kept in tick infested lots, pens, pastures or ranges shall be dipped regularly every two weeks in the same way and under the same requirements as for cattle, until released from state or federal quarantine."

> These are good laws. They require an owner to do what he should, in good conscience, want to do. Without regulation, some animal owners will have no mercy or compassion on God's creatures.

4-18. Transportation, etc., into state of ticky cattle, horses, mules, etc., prohibited.

"No ticky cattle, horses, mules or asses shall be driven, moved or transported in any way into a state."

> Here's a word you don't see every day—"ticky." That term of parlance, coined by our silver-haired legislators, applies to an animal with ticks on it. Call a six-foot tall, two hundred pounder "ticky" and you would thereafter carry your front teeth around in a Tupperware bowl.

4-19. County to Indemnify Owners of Cattle for Injuries Caused by Dipping.

"The county commission may, in its discretion, indemnify from the funds of such county the owners of cattle for injuries, damages or deaths caused by the dipping of such cattle in compliance with the laws of the state and the rules and regulations of the state board of agriculture and industries; provided, that such injuries, damages or deaths have been caused by the failure or negligence of the regularly qualified inspector commissioned by the state board of agriculture and industries to see that the arsenical solution used in the dipping vat is not over the standard of strength recommended by the United States Bureau of Animal Industry."

> This statute deals with dipping ticky cattle in an arsenic solution. So, when the county has caused cattle to be dipped and the cattle get sick or die, the county may pay damages to the owner. It should be noted, however, that when a governmental body has the option to pay or not, at its discretion, one should not hold one's breath.

4-20. Use of false or misleading advertising by public hatcheries and chick dealers or jobbers.

> Schools are under funded, property taxes kept too low to do any good (because the timber industry dictates to the legislatures), yet here is an ironclad law preventing misleading advertising in the sale of baby chicks.

4-21. Rabbits and chicks, ducklings, or other fowl; sale, etc., as pets or novelties.

"It shall be unlawful for any person, firm or corporation to display, sell, offer for sale barter or give away any baby rabbits, or baby chicks, ducklings or other fowl, but not including parrots, parakeets and canaries, as pets or novelties, regardless of whether or not such rabbits or fowl are dyed, colored or otherwise artificially treated.

Whoever violates this section is guilty of a misdemeanor and, upon conviction thereof, shall be punished as prescribed by law."

Prohibiting Artificial Coloring and Sale of Certain Animals and Fowls; Construction.

> "(1) It is unlawful for any person to dye or color artificially any animal or fowl, including but not limited to rabbits, baby chickens, and ducklings, or to bring any dyed or colored animal or fowl into this state.
>
> (2) It is unlawful for any person to sell, offer for sale, or give away as merchandising premiums, baby chickens, ducklings, or other fowl under 4 weeks of age or rabbits under 2 months of age to be used as pets, toys or retail premiums.
>
> (3) This section shall not be construed to apply to any animal or fowl, including but not limited to rabbits, baby chickens, and ducklings to be used or raised for agricultural purposes by persons with proper facilities to care for them or for poultry or livestock exhibitions.

(4) Any person violating the provisions of this section shall, upon conviction, be guilty of a misdemeanor of the second degree, punishable as provided in Section 775-082 or Section 773.083."

> This law is probably violated on an annual basis more than any other law on the books, except driving under the influence.

> It is illegal for any person to sell, barter, or give away any baby chicks, ducks, rabbits, or other fowl as a pet or novelty. It is illegal to dye or artificially color any chick, duckling or rabbit or other animal. Every Easter, however, thousands of parents buy baby rabbits, chicks, and ducks for their children. This is a good law, because tiny, loving hands can unwittingly squeeze the life out of such animals. For some reason, parrots, parakeets, and canaries are exempted from the anti-squeeze law. Perhaps the sharp beak on these fowl allows them a defense—and besides, they can fly.

4-22. Feeding of garbage to swine.

"It shall be unlawful for any person, municipality, county, political subdivision, governmental agency or department, institution, individual, partnership, corporation, association, other entity or organization to feel garbage to swine."

> This is a foresighted law that seeks to prevent outbreaks of E. coli and other microbes capable of causing life-threatening illnesses. A good veterinarian will tell you that the no garbage rule applies to dogs as well.

4-23. Possession, sale, etc. of hog cholera virus.

"It shall be unlawful for any person, firm, corporation or association in the state to have in possession or keep, sell or offer for sale, barter, exchange, give away or otherwise dispose of hog cholera virus."

> This law is a real teaser. It is comparable to a similar law that makes it illegal to possess the rabies virus.

> Must one be told not to try to brush a rattlesnake's teeth?

4-24. Keeping cockpit; cockfighting.

"Any person who keeps a cockpit or who in any public place fights cocks shall, on conviction, be fined not less than $20.00 nor more than $50.00."

> This so-called sport is classified as only a misdemeanor in Alabama, and is still legal in Louisiana.

4-25. Underground stables.

These laws are found wherever coal mines exist.

"No underground stables shall be constructed or used in coal mines after August 12, 1949, and straw for bedding or hay for feeding animals shall not be sent into coal mines. This does not apply to mines stabling animals underground on August 12, 1949. Rules for preventing fires and for maintenance of such stables and for handling straw and hay shall be prescribed in writing by the chief. Failure to comply with these rules shall constitute a violation of this chapter."

> The thought that horses and mules were kept in underground stables is chilling, but a glimpse of the victims of this centuries-old practice would break our hearts. White mules were most commonly used because they were more visible in the dark.

> I remember riding through a small hamlet of squatters near what is now Riverchase, Alabama. Their mules, all originally white, were smeared black with the indelible soot that comes from coal smoke.
>
> In long hollows leading up to the Cahaba River, near Birmingham, one can find a ten- to twenty-inch layer of coal dust under the pine straw, indicating the site of a coal wash. And in sinkholes and air vents, coal fires from the last century still burn underground.

4-26. Standards as to volume of air.

"Sufficient air must be circulated and conducted through all entries, slopes, travel ways, working places, air courses and open abandoned areas to dilute, render harmless and carry off noxious and explosive gases emitted in the mine, including smoke from blasting, and shall be not less than 150 cubic feel per man per minute.

If mules or horses are used in a mine, 500 cubic per animal per minute must be provided in addition to the minimum volume specified for men."

> This is another old law relating to horses and mules in coalmines. There were numerous one-man (privately owned) coalmines along Birmingham's Cahaba River. As a teenager, I rode horseback along the then-clear river. There were pens of mules scattered among the dozens of cabins, as well as piles of mine cars and buckets near the mine's entrance—which never seemed much larger than the opening to a yellow jacket's nest.

4-27. Transportation of Animals in Mines.

"No driver or other person shall be permitted to descend or ascend a shaft with any horse or mule, unless the said horse or mule and such assistants as he may need shall accompany it in any case."

> Notwithstanding the horror of horses and mules condemned to live out their days in dark and dangerous mines, it seems the purpose of this law was is to protect men, mules, and mine operators.

4-28. Enumeration of Conditions, etc., Constituting Public Nuisances Menacing Public Health.

"The following things, conditions and acts, among others, are hereby declared to be public nuisances per se, menacing public health and unlawful:

Animals (including fish, birds, fowls insects), other than human beings, infected with or acting as, or likely to act as, conveyors of disease or infection whereby they are likely to become menaces to public health."

> From earliest civilization, humans have frequently regarded animals as having no nerve endings, no capacity to suffer, and no right to live. Hoof and mouth disease and other dread plagues have caused the widespread destruction of animals only suspected of being diseased.

> Human life is of infinite value; however, it sometimes seems bizarre for a hospital to expend hundreds of thousands of dollars to treat a convicted murderer, repeat offender, or pedophile while a diseased animal is simply shot.

4-29. Polluting Public Water Supply.

"No person shall deposit any dead animal or fowl or any noxious, nauseous or poisonous substance or any human waste in any portion of a public water supply or in any private well, spring, reservoir, tank, vessel or receptacle appurtenant to a public or private water supply."

> Ghastly as it may sound, it took the passage of a criminal statute to discourage people from disposing of animal carcasses in wells, reservoirs, and other sources of potable water near a public or private water supply.

> Disposing of animals has always been a problem for farmers. I recall, as a child, helping my father heave dead calves off the precipice of Double Oak Mountain after a scourge of screwworm had decimated the herd.

4-30. Persons riding animals or driving animal-drawn vehicles.

"Every person riding an animal or driving any animal-drawn vehicle upon a roadway shall be granted all of the rights and shall be subject to all of the duties applicable to the driver of a vehicle by this chapter, except those provisions of this chapter, which by their very nature can have no application."

> This section of the law says persons riding horseback or in a vehicle pulled by a horse, mule, bull, ox, goat, or dog team have the same rights as motorists, and are subject to the same duties as well.

> In early Birmingham, all houses within the city had a shed for the family milk cow. Even as late as the 1950s there was the "Goatman," a kindly, old, round-faced African-American gentleman with snow-white hair and beard. He would hitch six or eight goats to a wooden wagon that

> had tall wooden-spoked wheels and was as big as a boxcar. For ten cents, kids could hurdle up onto a bench seat and be pulled around the paved and unpaved streets on summer Saturday mornings.

4-31. Uniform Certificate of Title Act.

"Exemptions: No Certificate of Title need be obtained for a vehicle moved solely by animal power. The provisions of Sections 32-5-246 through 32-5-251 shall not apply to bicycles or to ridden animals."

> "No tag for the nag;" that is, titles of ownership are not required for beasts of burden. I am thankful that states did not require branding in lieu thereof.

4-32. Lien Declared: For Stud Services.

"The owner of every stallion, jack, bull, ram, he-goat or boar, who keeps it for profit and charges a price for the service thereof, shall have a lien, for the amount of the stipulated price thereof, on any mare, jenny, cow, eye, she-goat or sow, to which such stallion, jack, bull, ram, he-goat or boar is put, and also on the colt, calf, lambs, kids or pigs born next after such service or contract therefore, and such lien shall be paramount to, and have precedence over, all other liens on the colt, calf, lambs, kids or pigs born next after such service, and within the proper period of gestation."

> Banks, builders, mechanics, attorneys, and shopkeepers have, under the law, a declared lien upon their work product. So it is that our legislatures, historically peopled with folks in agriculture, provided a lien for owners of male animals who are let out for stud services. This lien covers the offspring of the union, which, at the time of its birth, is in the possession of the owner of the female animal.

> One of the few breeds of animals that began with a single individual was the Morgan Horse. A horse named Figure, born in Massachusetts in 1789, was such a biologically distinct and physically superior creature that neighbors began soliciting the stallion for stud service. It was thus that the registered, purebred breed was begun.

4-33. Lien on stock for pasturage or training.

"Any keeper, owner, operator or proprietor of any pasture kept for grazing stock or of any cattle or livestock feed or fattening lot, or any keeper, owner or proprietor of any stable for the development or training of horses, or any person who keeps, fattens, feeds, cares for, trains or develops any horse, horses, cattle or livestock for another shall have a lien on all such horses, cattle or livestock so kept, fed, pastured, trained, cared for, fattened or developed by him, or under his control, for the payment of his charges for keeping, feeding, pasturing, training, caring for, fattening or developing the same, and he shall have the right to retain such horse, horses, cattle, livestock or stock, or so many thereof as may be necessary for the payment of such charges."

> The owner of lush pasturage or perhaps a livery stable has a lien on the animals he has cared for. If the landowner is not paid, then he is required to post notices at three conspicuous places in the county notifying the animal owner (lienee) that in ten days the animals may be sold to satisfy pasturage fees.

4-34. Animal sales between sunset and sunrise

"Any person who shall sell or buy any domestic animal or domestic fowl between the hours of sunset and sunrise shall be guilty of a misdemeanor and, upon conviction, shall be fined not less than $50.00 nor more than $500.00 and may also be sentenced to hard labor for the county for a period not exceeding one year; provided, however, that this section shall not apply to merchants, grocers or market men, who have a fixed place of business, selling to consumers, when the sales are made at such place of business."

> There they go again. Those crack legislators of ours have tackled a problem of doomsday proportions. The prohibition of the sale of any domestic animal or domestic fowl between sunset and sunrise is hereby announced.

4-35. Choking, glanders, etc.; sale, etc., of afflicted horse or mule.

"Any person who, by himself or another or as agent for another, shall knowingly sell or exchange any horse or mule subject to the disease or affliction known as "choking," or affected with glanders or some other fatal, contagious or infectious disease must, on conviction, be fined not less than $100.00 nor more than $500.00 and may also be sentenced to hard labor for the county for not less than three nor more than six months. one half of the fine shall go to the party injured. For each conviction under this section, the district attorney shall be entitled to a fee of $50.00."

> Glanders is really an awful disease. It causes the jaws to swell and the nostrils to discharge a massive volume of mucous. It is communicable to humans.

> This is possibly the only charge Kenneth Starr did not lodge against President Clinton.

4-36. Mares or jennets subject to lien.

"Any person who, with a knowledge of the lien, sells or otherwise disposes of any mare or jennet before the stipulated price for the service of any stallion or jack, for which a lien. is given by law, is paid must, on conviction, be fined not more than $100.00.

> The sale of a mare or jennet which is subject to a lien held by the owner of a servicing sire, is punishable by a $100.00 fine."
>
> I suppose that owning a ticky jennet would warrant death by firing squad.

4-37. Teeth of horse or mule; tampering.

"Any person burning, cauterizing or mechanically changing the natural appearance or condition of the teeth of any horse, mule or other soliped [an animal without a cloven hoof] in order to fraudulently make such animal appear younger than the animal really is shall be guilty of a misdemeanor.

Anyone who sells a horse, mule or other soliped who shall have burned or cauterized the teeth, in order to make the animal look younger, is guilty of a misdemeanor."

> I doubt that horses' teeth could accidentally get burned.

4-38. Teeth of horse or mule; evidence of tampering.

"The evidence required for the conviction of any person violating any provision of Section 3-1-23 must be substantiated as to the burning, cauterizing or changing of natural appearance or condition of the teeth of such horse, mule or other soliped by a graduate licensed veterinarian and, when necessary, the State Veterinarian or a graduate veterinarian selected by the State Veterinarian shall determine and testify to the changes that have been made in the teeth of such animal or animals."

> If the teeth of a horse, mule, or other soliped have apparently been altered, this fact is to be verified by a licensed veterinarian. This is prima facie evidence. Wyatt Earp was the last lawman to enforce this law.

4-39. Teeth of horse or mule; evidence of intent.

"The possession of any horse, mule or other soliped which has had its teeth burned, cauterized or mechanically changed in order to make such animal appear younger than it really is shall be prima facie evidence of intent to violate the provisions of this Section."

> The possession of a horse, mule or other soliped with altered or burned teeth is prima facie evidence of intent to violate the law.

> Here we have a prime cause of overcrowding in prisons.

4-40. Teeth of horse or mule; transportation of animal in violation.

"Any person transporting or moving into the state, for any purpose whatsoever, any horse, mule or other soliped which has had its teeth burned, cauterized or changed in any manner to make such animal appear younger than it really is shall be guilty of a misdemeanor.

The transportation of a horse, mule or other soliped into the state with altered or burned teeth is prima facie evidence of criminal intent."

4-41. Brands and marks; unlawful imposition or alteration

"Any person who, with intent to defraud, marks or brands any unmarked horse, mule, cow, hog, sheep, goat or other domestic animal which is the property of another or alters or defaces the mark or brand of such animal must, on conviction, be punished as if he had stolen it.

Any person who with intent to defraud, alters the brand of a horse, cow, mule, pig, goat, sheep, shall be punished as if he stole the animal."

4-42. Dead animals; disposal.

"All owners or custodians of animals which die or are killed in their possession or custody, other than such as are slaughtered for food, within 24 hours shall cause the bodies of such animals to be burned or buried at least two feet below the surface of the ground. Hogs dying from cholera or any other disease whatsoever shall be burned. No such animal shall be burned or buried sufficiently near a residence or residences as to create a nuisance. Any person violating this section, whether by failure to burn or bury an animal dying or being killed in his possession or by causing the same to be burned in such proximity to a dwelling or in such other way as to become a nuisance shall be guilty of a misdemeanor and, on conviction, shall be fined not more than $50.00."

> I had a bachelor uncle who was a veterinarian. In the fifties, the U.S. government hired him to go into Mexico and vaccinate cattle for an epidemic of hoof and mouth disease. He told me there was not as much vaccinating to do as there was burning of carcasses.

4-43. Depositing dead animals or fowl in running streams.

"Any person who deposits the body of a dead animal or fowl in any running stream must, on conviction, be fined $10.00, and one half of the fine must go to the informer."

> Consider this: Silas collects a crisp five-dollar bill for squealing on his next-door neighbor, Caleb, for chunking a dead duck into the creek. In times past, and to some degree even now, Silas would have to go into the Witness Protection Program to escape the wrath of Caleb.

4-44. Duties generally; maintenance, inspection and copying of reports of investigations of state toxicologist; police authority of state toxicologist and assistants.

"It shall be the further duty of the state toxicologist to cooperate with the commissioner of agriculture and industries and the state veterinarian in their investigations of deaths of domestic animals in cases of suspected criminal poisoning of such animals.

It shall be the further duty of the state toxicologist to cooperate with the commissioner of agriculture and industries and the state veterinarian in their investigations of deaths of domestic animals in cases of suspected criminal poisoning of such animals. The state toxicologist shall perform such other duties as are prescribed by the governor or the attorney general.

The state toxicologist and his designated assistants shall exercise the same police authority as any deputy sheriff or highway patrolman in the state."

> This is an important law for animal owners. It even gives toxicologists the police powers of a highway patrolman in investigating a poisoning death. Is it a good law?

> Poisoning is a singularly heinous method of killing something. In my home state of Alabama, hunters and farmers have perfected a particularly loathsome method for killing coyotes. Because coyotes are not protected by law (much like starlings, crows, and sparrows), not only their killing, but also the method of killing, is unregulated.

> Most good ol' Alabama boys saturate beef bones in antifreeze for up to a week. Then they scatter the bones in areas where coyotes are believed to nest. Ask any veterinarian, and you will learn that this glycol-type poisoning is painful, slow, and almost always fatal. Dogs, of course, as well as pigs, raccoons, possums, eagles, hawks, and other animals often get to the poisoned bait first. The lethal recipe is an equal opportunity form of terrorism, killing all who sample.

Chapter Five

Wild Animals—Their Protection

"Are not two sparrows sold for a farthing? And one of them shall not fall on the ground without your Father,"

Matthew 10:29

5-1. Permits for collection of wild animals, birds, etc., for scientific purposes, etc.

"No person shall at any time collect any protected wild animal or bird or egg of any bird in this state for propagation or scientific purposes except under the direction, supervision and regulation of the commissioner of conservation and natural resources, who, on the payment of $1.00, may issue such propagation or scientific permits annually to properly accredited persons or institutions. Any person, firm, association or corporation being or having in possession at any time such animal or bird or the eggs of such bird without a permit as provided in this section shall be guilty of a misdemeanor and, upon conviction therefore, shall be punished by a fine of not less than $10.00 nor more than $25.00 for each offense."

> This is a conservation-oriented law requiring an individual to obtain a permit from the Department of Conservation before collecting wild birds, animals, or bird's eggs.

> During World War II, soldiers faced a worldwide shortage of hen's eggs. Over one thousand types of bird's eggs were tested, and only one type actually tasted like a hen's egg. It was the product of a black tipped gull found in the Bahamas and certain other Caribbean islands. I've eaten these little eggs and they are quite good.

5-2. Possession, sale, purchase, etc., of protected wild birds, etc.

"Any person, firm, association or corporation who takes, catches, kills or has in possession at any time, living or dead, any protected wild bird not a game bird or who sells or offers for sale, buys, purchases or offers to buy or purchase any such bird or exchange same for anything of value or who shall sell or expose for sale or buy any part of the plumage, skin or body of any bird protected by the laws of this state or who shall take or willfully destroy the nests of any wild bird or who shall have such nests or eggs of such birds in his possession, except as otherwise provided by law, shall be guilty of a misdemeanor and, upon conviction, shall be punished by a fine of not less than $10.00 nor more than $25.00 for each offense."

> It is also illegal to possess any skin, feathers, or other part of any wild, protected bird or its nest. In Guatemala, for instance, there remains but a handful of the absolutely beautiful bird known as the quetzal. So popular and glorious was this bird that the Mayans captured it in order to worship it. (Incidentally, Guatemalans now use the name quetzal to denote their units of currency.) The incidence of such situations explains why protective laws must be passed.

5-3. Enumeration of birds not protected.

"English sparrows, crows and starlings are not protected by the game laws of this state and may be killed at any time."

> This is a foolish law, passed with absolutely no forethought. To license this bloodthirsty society to be able to annihilate a species is to threaten future generations with a situation similar to the eradication of the buffalo on the American plains. However, things could be worse. If sparrows, crows, and starlings were found to be a revolutionary new appetite suppressant, they would disappear as quickly as the Y2K issue.

Animals Not Protected:

Wolves and other predators are not protected by statute in several states. Texas and Arkansas have, for example, had statutes offering a bounty for the killing of certain animals considered predatory or harmful. In southeastern states, armadillos, coyote, and wild hogs have little, if any, statutory protection. Coyotes may be killed throughout the nation, as well as gophers, prairie dogs, and crows.

The Federal Endangered Species legislation has greatly curtailed this encouragement to kill. States have also passed similar laws of their own. Nevertheless, listed below are several statutes, still in the state codes, which offer bounties for killing certain animals.

Rattlesnakes, Wolves, Coyotes, Panthers, Bobcats, and Other Predatory Animals:

> "(a) The Commissioners Court of Aransas, Bee, Refugio, or San Patricio County may pay bounties for the destruction of rattlesnakes, wolves, coyotes, panthers, bobcats, and other predatory animals in the county to preserve game and to protect the interests of livestock and poultry raisers."

Commissioners Court May Purchase Poison:

> "(a) The commissioners court of a county may purchase poisons and related accessories required by citizens of the county to destroy prairie dogs, wildcats, gophers, ground squirrels, wolves, coyotes, rats, English sparrows, and ravens.

Angelina, Henderson, or Trinity County: Wolves and Other Predatory Animals:

> (a) The Commissioners Court of Angelina, Henderson, or Trinity County may pay bounties for the destruction of wolves and other predatory animals in the county."

Effect of Other Laws:

"This subchapter does not authorize:

(1) the killing of an animal if the killing is prohibited by federal or state law or rule; or

(2) the payment of a bounty for killing an animal if the killing prohibited by federal or state law or rule.

The revised law inserts a new provision for the reader's convenience to clarify the fact that the revised law does not authorize the killing of animals if the killing is otherwise unlawful or the payment of bounties for killing those animals. Several animals listed in the subchapter are endangered species, and the killing of endangered species is prohibited by federal as well as state law. (16 U.S.C. 1531 et seq., Chapter 68, Parks and Wildlife Code.) In addition, the Parks and Wildlife Code and rules adopted under that code govern the killing of fur-bearing, game, and non game animals. (Chapters 63, 67, and 71, Parks and Wildlife Code.)"

Bounty on Wolves:

"(a) The county court of any county of this state is authorized to pay a bounty for each wolf killed within the county when satisfactory proof has been made of the killing of the animals.

(b) The State of Arkansas shall pay to any person killing a wolf a bounty in the amount equal to the amount paid to the person by an county in this state under subsection (a) of this section. Payment shall be made from the Game Protection Fund of the Arkansas State Game and Fish Commission. However, the bounty paid by the commission shall not exceed fifteen dollars ($15.00) for each old wolf and five dollars ($5.00) for each wolf under six (6) months of age."

Emergency Clause Provided:

"Whereas, hawks and/or crows are exceedingly destructive to much of the farm lands in our State by killing barn yard fowls and causing a great amount of destruction, an emergency is hereby declared and this being necessary for the public peace, health and safety of public interest, it shall take effect and be in full force from and after its passage.

Whereas, Bob cats, commonly known as wild cats, gophers and/or wolves are destroying game birds and small livestock in many sections of the state, an emergency is hereby declared and this act being necessary for the public peace, health and safety, an emergency is hereby found and declared to exist and this act shall take effect and be in full force from and after its passage.

Whereas, the farmers of the State of Arkansas are suffering irreparable damage from wolves destroying cattle and other livestock, and this act being necessary for the immediate preservation of the public peach, health and safety an emergency is declared to exist, and this act shall be in full force and effect from and after its passage.

It is hereby found and determined by the General Assembly that fish and minnow farming is very important to the Arkansas economy, that the cormorant is inflicting serious hardship on fish and minnow farmers in the state by killing and consuming large quantities of pond raised fish and minnows; that there is no practical method of protect the fish and minnows from the large flocks of cormorant in the state; that this act is designed to correct this undesirable situation and should be given effect immediately. Therefore, an emergency is hereby declared to exist and this act being necessary for the preservation of the public peach, health and safety shall be in full force and effect from and after its passage and approval."

> States having statutes permitting or encouraging the killing of predatory or harmful animals have been required to limit or outlaw the species killing to some degree. The federal endangered species statutes and the outcry from animal rights groups have effected those changes.

> Until ten years ago, the full text of bounty statutes was in full force and effect. This situation can be illustrated by excerpts from two different state laws on wolverines. Both had statutes that allowed or encouraged the accelerated killing of wolverines—and both have been repealed.

The Alaska Statute reads: "Employment of hunters and trappers to suppress predatory animals; bounties on wolverines, wolves, and coyotes. Repealed, Section 29, Chapter 132 SLA 1984."

Minnesota Statute 97B.641 "Cougar and Wolverine. There is no open season for cougar or wolverine."

> This 1997 law replaces the previous 1986 law allowing unfettered killing of wolverines.

5-4. Taking, etc., of protected birds or animals at night; taking, etc., of raccoons or opossums at night; taking of foxes at night.

"It shall be unlawful, except as to trapping as otherwise provided by law, for a person to take, capture, or kill, or attempt to take, capture, or kill any bird or animal protected by the laws of this state between sunset and daylight of the following day, except that the Commissioner of Conservation and Natural Resources may by a duly promulgated regulation, allow the taking, catching, or killing of raccoons and opossums is permitted during nighttime hours by regulations of the commissioner, the animals only be legally taken with the use of a light and/or a shotgun using shot no larger than number eight, and the person or persons so hunting shall be accompanied by a dog or dogs and, if hunting on the lands of another, shall have the written permission of the landowner.

Any person violating this section shall be guilty of a misdemeanor and, upon conviction thereof, shall be punished for the first offense by a fine of not less than one thousand dollars $1,000) nor more than two thousand dollars $2,000 and the court shall revoke all hunting license privileges for a period of three years from the date of conviction. Any person shall be punished for the second and each subsequent offense by a fine of not less than two thousand dollars ($2,000 and shall have all hunting license privileges revoked for a period of three years from the date of conviction, and shall be imprisoned in the county jail for a period of not less than three days nor more than ten days.

No provision of this section shall be construed to prohibit the nighttime hunting of foxes with dogs."

> This is a good law in many respects, except the fox clause. I, personally, don't know anyone who leaves the peace and comfort of his living room to go barging into the deep woods at night with his tooth set on a fox. It is, however, a bad law if it allows the unrestricted killing of any species—which it does.

5-5. Hunting, etc., of or possession of protected birds or animals during closed season.

"Any person who hunts, takes, catches, captures, kills or has in his possession or who attempts to hunt, take, catch, capture or kill, any bird or animal protected by law or regulation of this state except during the open season when same may be hunted, taken, caught, captured or killed shall be guilty of a misdemeanor and, upon conviction, shall be punished by a fine of not less than $50.00 nor more than $500.00 and, at the discretion of the court, may also be imprisoned in the county jail for not longer than six months. Any person convicted the second time for violating this section shall be guilty of a misdemeanor and shall be punished by a fine of not less than $100.00 nor more than $500.00 and, at the discretion of the court, may also be imprisoned in the county jail for not longer than six months. Any person convicted for violating this section the third or subsequent times shall be guilty of a misdemeanor and shall be punished by a fine of not less than $250.00 nor more than $500.00 and, at the discretion of the court, may also be imprisoned in the county jail for not longer than six months. It is provided further that any person who hunts, takes, catches, captures, or kills, or attempts to hunt, take, catch, capture, or kill, a wild turkey in an illegal manner or during the closed hunting season, or has in his possession a wild turkey killed during the closed hunting season or taken in an illegal manner, shall be guilty of a misdemeanor and upon conviction shall be punished by a fine of not less than $250.00 nor more than $500.00 and, at the discretion of the court, may also be imprisoned in the county jail for not longer than six months."

> This is a law enacted for a good purpose; however, I doubt that any person short of Daniel Boone could ever find—much less shoot—a wild turkey at night.

5-6. Sale and purchase of game birds and animals including the meat or other product thereof.

"Any person, firm, or corporation who sells, offers, or exposes for sale, buys, purchases, barters, or exchanges anything of value for any game bird or game animal or any part thereof at any time shall be guilty of a misdemeanor and, upon conviction, shall be punished by a fine of not less than $150.00 nor more than $500.00 for each offense. Duly licensed catchers of fur-bearing animals may sell to regularly licensed buyers or dealers only the furs, skins, or pelts of fur-bearing animals which they lawfully take, capture, or kill. The licensed catcher of fur-bearing animals may sell or offer for sale for food the dressed carcass of edible fur-bearing animals named by law or regulations. However, notwithstanding anything herein to the contrary, it shall not be a violation of this section to sell, offer, or expose for sale, buy, purchase, barter, or exchange anything of value for any of the following: (1) Lawfully taken 'green' raw untanned deer hides and their hooves, squirrels' skins, hides, and tails; (2) Finished product items such as gloves, shoes, clothing, jewelry, tanned deer hides, and similar products; and (3) Labeled, prepackaged venison, etc."

> In Arizona and almost a dozen other states, any restaurant offering horse meat on the menu must have a sign on the premises printed in eight by three inch letters, as well as a green-colored notice on the menu, that advises patrons of the fact.

5-7. Hunting, etc., of wild turkeys with dogs.

"Any person who hunts, pursues, captures or kills a wild turkey in this state with the aid of a dog at any time shall be guilty of a misdemeanor and, upon conviction, shall be punished by a fine of not less than $25.00 nor more than $50.00 for each offense."

5-8. Hunting, etc., of wild turkey hens, female deer, antelope or elk, and unantlered male deer.

"Any person who hunts, pursues, captures, kills or who attempts to pursue, capture or kill any wild turkey hen or any doe or female deer, antelope, deer or elk or who kills an unantlered male any time shall be guilty of a misdemeanor and, upon conviction, shall be punished by a fine of not less than $50.00 nor more than $500.00 for each offense."

> Hunters will not tolerate the commission of this offense. Hunting clubs will turn in one of their own number who commits such a violation. Why is this so? Because the male of these legal species is invariably more secretive and wary than the female. (Anyone who has a teenage daughter knows exactly what I'm talking about.) Thus, the hen or doe is more visible—and can be killed more easily by hunters. Decimation of the breeding females leaves the males still secretive and difficult to spot, and that can lead to endangerment of the species. Hunters who pay for hunting rights know that the herd can increase in numbers (even though they must settle for fewer kills) if they target only legal males.

5-9. Taking, etc., of deer from public waters.

"It shall be unlawful for any person, firm or corporation to take or catch, by any means or device, deer, whether dead or alive, from the public waters."

> Persons not living in rural or forested areas might not be aware that will deer commonly—often daily—swim rivers and lakes. They swim well, but are not very fast. Cutthroat illegals ride the river in a boat with an outboard motor. If they spot a swimming deer, they motor up to it, cut its throat, put a noose on it, and pull it to shore.

5-10. Taking, etc., of deer, antelope, moose or elk at night.

"It shall be unlawful for any person, firm or corporation to take, capture or kill deer, antelope, moose or elk at night by any means or device, including but not limited to use of any type of light."

> Taking deer, elk, moose, or antelope at night is highly illegal, highly common, and completely cowardly. Deer freeze in place when a bright light is shined in their eyes. This practice goes on throughout the states, in and out of season. Game officers are so horribly outnumbered that the best they can usually do is find the butchered carcass the next day.

> This is serious business. Landowners have shot and killed night hunters. Night hunters have shot and killed game wardens. Attempting an armed robbery of the Federal Reserve Bank is a safer ploy.

5-10a. Protected Game: Antelope, moose, whitetail or mule deer, bear, elk, mountain lion, rocky mountain bighorn sheep, wild turkey, or subspecies—Hunting, selling, buying—Seizure of meat, head, hide or any part of animal by Conservation Officers.

"(1) No person, including but not limited to persons licensed for commercial hunting or wildlife breeders, may hunt, chase, capture, shoot, shoot at, wound, attempt to take or take, attempt to kill or kill, or slaughter an antelope, moose, whitetail or mule deer, sheep, wild turkey, or any subspecies except in open season under Section 5-401 of this code.

(2) No person shall sell, offer for sale or buy or offer to buy an antelope, moose, whitetail or mule deer, bear, elk, mountain lion, rocky mountain bighorn sheep, wild turkey, or any subspecies or any parts thereof, except as otherwise provided by rules prescribed by the Oklahoma Wildlife Conservation Commission or by law.

(3) The provisions of this subsection shall not be construed to prevent a hide, antlers or horns from illegally taken whitetail or mule deer, elk, moose, antelope or bighorn sheep from being sold or traded by a person who legally harvested or who legally possesses the hide, antlers or horns. Any antlers or horns sold or traded shall have been removed from the skull of the deer in such a way as to leave no portion of the skull attached.

B. (1) It shall be unlawful for any person to have in his possession any meat, head, hide or any part of the carcass of any wildlife not legally taken.

(2) Any meat, head, hide or any part of the carcass of any wildlife not legally taken shall be subject to immediate seizure by a game warden.

(3) The provisions of this subsection shall not apply to privately owned, domesticated animals so designated by the Oklahoma Wildlife Conservation Commission."

Moose Hunting Season:

"The Fish and Wildlife Board may establish a moose hunting season upon receipt of such a recommendation from the Commissioner. If such a season is declared, the following conditions shall apply:

A. Wildlife Management Units (W.M.U.) are established as described in Regulation #912.

(1) The Board may declare an open season for moose in one or more units in any given year.

B. Moose hunting season shall be held during the month of October."

5-11. Taking, etc., of protected birds or animals by means of bait.

"No person at any time shall take, catch, kill or attempt to take, catch or kill any bird or animal protected by law or regulation of the state by means, aid or use, directly or indirectly, of any bait such as shelled, shucked or unshucked corn or of wheat or other grain, salt or any other feed whatsoever that has been so deposited, placed, distributed or scattered as to constitute for such birds or animals a lure, attraction or enticement to, on or over the area where such hunter or hunters are attempting to kill or take them; provided, that such birds or animals may be taken under properly shucked corn and standing crops of corn, wheat or other grain or feed and grains scattered solely as a result of normal agricultural harvesting and provided further, migratory birds may be hunted [only] under the most recent provisions established by the U.S. Fish and Wildlife Service or regulations promulgated by the commissioner of the department of conservation and natural resources within the limits of the federal regulations."

> This code section tracks a federal law that protects migratory birds. The grey dove migrates annually from Mexico to the United States. Hence, hunting dove over a baited field is a violation of federal law. It is also considered the least sportsmanlike act imaginable by true bird hunters. Regrettably, people return from Mexico and Central America with stories of having shot fifteen hundred to three thousand doves in five days. Mexico needs to pass and enforce a law similar to ours in order to truly protect this bird.

5-12. Unlawful methods of hunting birds or animals protected by law or regulations.

"No person shall at any time make use of any pitfall, deadfall, baited field, cage, trap, net, pen, baited hook, snare, poison, explosive, or chemical for the purpose of injuring, capturing, or killing birds or animals protected by law or regulation of this state. This section shall not prevent the trapping of animals classified as fur-bearing animals by a duly licensed fur catcher. It shall be legal to use a scaffold for gun hunting of all legal game species except wild turkey and to use a scaffold for bow hunting of all legal game species."

> The scaffold referred to in the above code section is known throughout the U.S. as a tree stand. Regrettably, many a numb, cold hunter, having liberally imbibed Old Coot to fend off frostbite while sitting in his tree stand in winter, has proceeded to fall out and down. This, in turn, has spawned lawsuits against tree stand manufacturers. Sporadic recoveries of damages do occur. Often, the manufacturer consists of two or three guys, a welding torch, and a pick-up truck filled with pipe.

5-13. "Pen-raised quail" defined.

"A pen-raised quail is a quail which has been hatched from an egg laid by a quail confined in a pen or coop and has itself been wholly raised in a pen or coop by a duly licensed quail breeder holding a permit as provided by this article from the state department of conservation and natural resources."

5-14. Fowl to be hunted; minimum stock released for hunting.

"Game which may be hunted on a preserve licensed under this article shall be artificially propagated or 'pen-raised' bobwhite, quail, pheasants, chukar partridge and such other species of fowl as the commissioner of conservation and natural resources shall designate. A minimum stock of at least 1,000 bobwhite quail, if bobwhite quail are to be hunted on the preserve, or a minimum stock of 200 of each of the other species of birds, listed above, to be hunted on a licensed preserve shall be released on the licensed hunting area during each hunting period."

> Birds raised in captivity never become fully wild, even after release. Thus, foxes, raccoons, and coyotes decimate the bulk of the near tame birds if they are not hunted rather soon after release.

5-15. License required; rules and regulations.

"Any person, firm, or corporation desiring to operate a hunting or shooting preserve commercially on which artificially propagated birds may be hunted, taken, captured, killed, harvested or otherwise recovered, may do so upon obtaining a hunting preserve license and complying with the provisions of this article and all rules and regulations promulgated by the commissioner of Conservation and Natural Resources governing the operation of hunting preserves."

> Here's a law regulating a sport for rich, famous, and generally egotistical people who like to win. Pen-raised quail are fed until they are grown. Then they are released hours before a scheduled big hunt. The sportsmen, conducted by top pedigree bird dogs, proceed to fire away at these birds who have been known to fly, startled, toward the gunfire—even occasionally landing on a gun barrel. This sport, in terms of necessary prowess and skill, is similar to catching Maine lobsters in the tank in the grocery store.

5-16. Hunting licenses required of preserve patrons; seven-day license; operators as agent vendors of licenses.

"(a) Hunting licenses shall be required of all persons hunting on licensed hunting preserves. Residents shall be licensed under the regularly established game laws. Each nonresident hunting on a licensed preserve shall be required to possess a regular nonresident annual hunting license or a nonresident trip hunting license.

(b) In lieu of a regular hunting license as provided in subsection a), either a resident or a nonresident may purchase a seven-day commercial fowl hunting preserve license that allows that person the privilege of hunting only artificially propagated or pen-raised fowl as designated by the Commissioner of Conservation and Natural Resources as legal to hunt on a licensed commercial fowl hunting preserve. The cost of a seven-day commercial fowl hunting preserve license shall be $8.00, plus a $2.00 issuance fee. The license shall be valid for seven consecutive days from the date of issuance."

> The above statute is typical in all respects except the costs of licenses. Many states have set costs much higher than those in this example.

5-17. Licenses on Weekends.

"To better serve the public and in order that the state will not lose revenue from the loss of sale of licenses to out-of-state visitors arriving on weekends, each hunting preserve operator licensed pursuant to this article shall be an agent vendor of all nonresident and resident hunting licenses with any issuance fees collected therefore to be remitted to the judge of probate of the county in which the preserve is located."

> This is a service useful to out-of-state hunters who would otherwise have to wait until Monday for the courthouse to open.

5-18. Enforcement of game and fish laws; inspection of preserves.

"Duly authorized agents of the state department of conservation and natural resources, game wardens and other law enforcement officers duly authorized to enforce game and fish laws shall have authority to enforce all game and fish laws and regulations on such preserves; and for such purposes are authorized to enter and inspect licensed hunting preserves."

> The powers granted under this section come close to violating our Fourth Amendment rights of freedom from search and seizure. The necessity of protecting wild animals, as well as the fact that hunting is a privilege granted by the states, allow this power to be authorized.

5-19. Definitions.

"Whenever used in this article, the following words and terms shall have the following respective meaning unless the context clearly indicates otherwise:

>(1) MIGRATORY WATERFOWL. Any wild duck, wild goose, brant or coot (poule d'eau).

>(2) DEPARTMENT. State department of conservation and natural resources.

>(3) STAMP. The state migratory waterfowl stamp furnished by the department."

5-20. Construction of article; purpose thereof.

"This article shall be construed in furtherance of the purpose thereof, which is to insure the procurement, development, restoration, maintenance or preservation of wetlands for migratory waterfowl habitat."

5-21. Stamp required for hunting migratory waterfowl; form; procedure.

"A person shall not hunt migratory waterfowl within this state or its waters without first procuring a state migratory waterfowl stamp and having such stamp in his possession validated by his signature written across the face of the stamp in ink while hunting or taking migratory waterfowl. The form of the stamp shall be determined by the department and the department shall furnish the stamps to the judge of probate or issuing officer of the counties for issuance or sale in the same manner as state hunting licenses are issued or sold."

5-22. Issuance of stamp; cost; disposition of issuing fees.

"A stamp shall be issued to each hunting license applicant upon written request to the judge of probate or issuing officer of any county of the state on forms provided by the department and the payment of a fee of five dollars. Each stamp shall be valid for the duration of one hunting season as established by the department. Stamps shall be available for sale prior to any waterfowl season, including any special season which may precede the regular season."

> These stamps are commonly referred to as duck stamps.

"The judge of probate or issuing officer shall be allowed a fee of $.25 for each such license issued by him, which issuing fee shall be in addition to the cost of the stamp. In counties where the probate judge or issuing officer is on the fee system, the issuing fee shall be retained by the probate judge or issuing officer, and in counties where the probate judge or issuing officer is on a salary basis, the fee shall be paid by him into the county treasury to the credit of the appropriate fund."

> The above section provides fertile ground for over-enforcement or selective enforcement, depending on whether the judge of probate keeps the fees or passes them on to the county.

5-23. Dog trainer's license.

"(a) All persons engaging in the business of training dogs for hunting or field trial purposes for remuneration or profit shall first procure a dog trainer's license from the department of conservation and natural resources and pay for same the sum of $5.00, such license to be procured and such fees to be deposited in like manner as provided for other licenses set forth in this article.

(b) Any person in this state who trains dogs for hunting or field trial purposes for remuneration or profit without first procuring from the department of conservation and natural resources a dog trainer's license shall be guilty of a misdemeanor and, on conviction, shall be punished by fine of not less than $15.00 nor more than $25.00 for each offense."

> Once again, it should be noted that the fees specified in this statute are among the lowest in the United States.

5-24. When dogs permitted in areas; liability of owners of dogs at large in areas

"No dog shall be permitted except on leash within any wildlife management area except in accordance with the rules and regulations promulgated by the commissioner conservation and natural resources, and whoever shall be the owner of any dog at large within any wildlife management area shall be guilty of a misdemeanor."

> Dogs are known to "run" big game (chase the animals until they are exhausted, killing them), and many states include such an act under those of a dangerous dog, which allows the dog to be killed by a conservation officer.

5-25. Impoundment of dogs; redemption or destruction of impounded dogs.

"The commissioner of conservation and natural resources shall cause to be constructed within each wildlife management area a building or enclosure suitable for the impoundment of dogs found upon said wildlife management area in violation of section 9-11-305. Whenever a dog is found upon said wildlife management area in violation of section 9-11-305, it shall be impounded in said building or enclosure until such time as it is redeemed by its owner or is destroyed in accordance with the provisions of this section."

5-26. Opening or closing of season for killing of beaver.

"Whenever the commissioner of conservation and natural resources determines that a reduction in the number of beavers is necessary to the public health and welfare of people of this state or for the preservation of the species or to prevent serious damage resulting from the damming or diversion of public streams by beavers, said commissioner of conservation and natural resources shall be authorized to open or close a season in any county area or section of state for the killing of beavers and to provide for payment of a bounty of $5.00 for each beaver killed."

> This is another example of a bounty on a wild animal.

5-27. Liability for injury or damage to persons or domestic animals of persons using traps, etc., to take, capture, etc., fur-bearing.

"Any person shall be strictly liable for civil damages who causes the injury or damage to any person or domestic animal as a result of using any trap or similar device to take, capture or kill any of the fur-bearing animals protected by the laws or regulations of this state.

Any person who suffers injury or damage to his person or domestic animal as a result of such activity shall have an action for civil damages and such aggrieved person need not prove negligence."

> A person, pet or domesticated animal injured or damaged by a trap is automatically entitled to recover damages from the trapper without the need to prove fault on the trapper's part.

> A man I know in Georgia pays ten thousand dollars—annually—to have a crew dynamite beaver dams on his three-thousand-acre farm to prevent the flooding of his fields.

5-28. Seizure, forfeiture and disposal of prohibited devices, etc., used in catching, killing, etc., fish or fur-bearing animals.

"It shall be the duty of the commissioner of conservation and natural resources or any of his wardens or agents to seize all instruments or devices prohibited by or constructed contrary to law and used unlawfully in trapping, capturing and killing fur-bearing animals in this state, as well as all instruments or devices prohibited by or constructed contrary to law and used unlawfully in taking, catching, or killing fish in the public streams or waters of this state and after such seizure to hold the same for evidence."

> Trapping, by virtue of its elements of torture and painful death, is strictly regulated. Trappers consequently operate under the protection of no more laws than a legislature can tolerate. Starlings and trappers are about equal under the law.

"(b) In all cases of arrests and convictions for the use of such unlawful or illegal instruments or devices, such instruments or devices are declared to be a nuisance and shall be carried before the court having jurisdiction of such offense, and said court shall order such instruments or devices forfeited to the department of conservation and natural resources immediately after trial and conviction of the person in whose possession such devices or instruments were found. When any illegal instrument or device prohibited by this section is found and the owner of same shall not be known to the officer finding same, such officer shall procure from the judge of any court having jurisdiction an order forfeiting said instrument or device to the department of conservation and natural resources."

> Many animal rescue organizations have periodic trap-burnings. This is most commendable; however, I can't understand how a steel trap can catch fire.

5-29. Trapping on or from right-of-way of state highway.

"It shall be unlawful for anyone to trap on or from a state highway right-of-way unless the trapper has the permission of adjoining landowners."

5-30. Checking of traps; hanging or suspending of bait over or within 25 feet of steel trap.

"All traps set in or beneath water must be checked at least once every 72 hours. All traps other than water sets must be checked at least once every 24 hours. [Since animals can't hold their breath for more than a few minutes, this law accomplishes nothing.] It shall be unlawful for anyone to hang or suspend bait over or within 25 feet of a steel trap."

5-31. Authority to prohibit importation of birds, animals, fish, etc.

"(a) The commissioner of conservation and natural resources is hereby empowered to prohibit by duly promulgated regulation the importation of any bird, animal, reptile, amphibian or fish when the importation of such animal, bird, reptile, amphibian or fish would not be in the best interest of the state.

(b) The provisions of this section shall not apply to birds, animals, reptiles, amphibians and fish used for display purposes for carnivals, zoos, circuses and other like shows and exhibits where ample provision is made so that such birds, animals reptiles, amphibians and fish will not escape or be released in this state."

> Someone obviously had his back turned when a teenager in an eastern state recently added a black mamba snake to his collection. The black mamba, which has since escaped into the environs, is known in its natural habitat of Africa as the "one-hundred-foot snake," because a person who has been bitten by it can go no more than one hundred feet before dying from the bite.

"(c) Any person, firm, corporation, partnership or association who or which imports, brings or causes to be brought or imported into the state bird, animal, reptile, amphibian or fish, the importation of which has been forbidden by duly promulgated regulation of the commissioner of conservation and natural resources, shall be in violation of the provisions of this section and upon conviction thereof shall be fined not less than $50.00 nor more than $250.00 for each offense."

> This law, which prohibits the importation of foreign species, is very important. Sportsmen or businesses have introduced different species over the years that have had irreversible effects on the U.S. ecosystem. Walking catfish, Indiana minnows, and zebra mussels are harmful and voracious invaders that have no indigenous predators. I shall use my home state of Alabama to illustrate.

> Some state-specific examples of the proliferation of not-natural species are the coyote, the red wolf, the armadillo, the tilapia, the feral cat, and the alligator. Twenty years ago, there were no coyotes east of the Mississippi. Alabama's code of law never contained the word coyote, because none existed in the state. Then, somehow, the critters crossed the Mississippi. They presently constitute an ecological epidemic, and can be found in all sixty-seven counties. They are so prevalent and difficult to remove that a posh residential section atop Birmingham's

Red Mountain has paid a shaman fifty thousand dollars to banish the beasts.

The red wolf was introduced into a Federal Park in Barbour County by the U.S. government, under controlled conditions (i.e., only a limited number of animals were brought in, each animal was tagged, and its habits were monitored). So far, the introduction of the red wolf has only minimally impacted the native bird population.

The armadillo had always lived in the lower four Alabama counties. Then, due to global warming or some other phenomenon, they suddenly moved north. They are plenteous all the way to the Tennessee line.

The tilapia is a breed of fish introduced by the Department of Conservation to feed upon the menace of duckweed. Biologists certified that the animals could not reproduce, would not bite a hook, and were not a table food. Because they are in fact delicious, anglers are glad they bite a hook. Incidentally, they reproduce rather well.

The alligator was, for thousands of years, confined to only three extreme southern counties of Alabama. Again, the rise in temperature of about one-half degree over the last twenty years may account for the gators presence in some forty counties.

Feral cats are house cats that are lost or abandoned and take on wild characteristics. They can be found in every state and often breed with wildcats or bobcats.

Hawaii, incidentally, provides that any new species introduced legally into the state may not be hunted for ten years.

5-32. Release of turkeys into wild areas of state prohibited; exceptions; penalty.

"(a) It shall be unlawful to release any tame turkey, or any other turkey, whether wild or tame, into any of the wild areas of this state.

(b) The provisions of this section shall not apply to any turkeys kept by any farmer or homeowner of this state for normal agricultural purposes or for personal consumption..

(c) Nothing in this section is intended to prohibit the stocking of wild turkeys by authorized personnel of the department of conservation and natural resources for propagation or research purposes.

(d) Any person who shall be convicted of violating any provision of this section shall be deemed guilty of a 'violation' under the criminal code of this state and shall be punished as provided for in said code."

> The release of wild turkeys into wild areas of the state could obviously cause some type of ecological imbalance. With crime what it is in some of our cities, I'm not clear as to which areas are considered wild.

5-33 Wild Animals Are the Property of the State.

> Who owns the deer, buffalo, squirrels, or bobcats? The vast majority of states prohibit private persons from owning or possessing wild animals native to that state. Exotic, nonnative species, such as tigers or elephants (animals ferae naturae), may be owned or possessed only with a specific permit or license that carries regulations regarding fencing and other such specifics.

Personal Possession of Wildlife.

"(1) It is unlawful for any person or persons to possess any wildlife as defined in this act, whether indigenous to Florida or not, until she or he has obtained a permit as provided by this section from the Fish and Wildlife Conservation Commission.

(2) The classifications of types of wildlife and fees to be paid for the issuance of permits shall be as follows:

(a) Class I—Wildlife which, because of its nature, habits, or status, shall not be possessed as a personal pet.

(b) Class II—Wildlife considered to present a real or potential threat to human safety, the sum of $100.00 per annum.

(3) The commission shall promulgate regulations defining Class I and II types of wildlife. The commission shall also establish regulations and requirements necessary to insure that permits are granted only to persons qualified to possess and care properly for wildlife and that permitted wildlife possessed as personal pets will be maintained in sanitary surroundings and appropriate neighborhoods.

(4) In instances where wildlife is seized or taken into custody by the commission, said owner or possessor of such wildlife shall be responsible for payment of all expenses relative to the capture, transport, boarding, veterinary care, or other costs associated with or incurred due to seizure or custody of wildlife. Such expenses shall be paid by said owner or possessor upon any conviction or finding of guilt of a criminal or non criminal violation, regardless of adjudication of plea entered, of any provision of chapter 828 or this chapter, or rule of the commission or if such violation is disposed of under Section 921.187."

States allowing ownership of wild species include:

Idaho, where persons may own wild mammals other than big game species.

Wisconsin, Georgia, and Illinois have laws stating that wild animals belong to the state until legally reduced to the possession of a person.

Montana's law states that upon capture of a bear, wolf, mountain lion, tiger, or coyote, it must be tattooed before release. (Yes, tigers are mentioned.) So capture is allowed, but not ownership. I doubt that persons capturing bears, wolves, mountain lions, or tigers could boast a large constituency. It would seem that the widows of these daring souls would constitute a group of sufficient numbers to start a third political party.

(Temporary) Restitution for Illegal Killing or Possession of Certain Wildlife.

"(1) Except as provided in 87-1-115 and in addition to other penalties provided by law, a person convicted or forfeiting bond or bail upon a charge of the illegal taking, killing, or possession of a wild bird, mammal, or fish listed in this section shall reimburse the state for each bird, mammal, or fish according to the following schedule:

(a) bighorn sheep, grizzly bear, and endangered species, $2,000.00;

(b) elk, caribou, bald eagle, black ear, and moose, $1,000.00;

(c) mountain lion, lynx, wolverine, buffalo, golden eagle, osprey, falcon, antlered deer as defined by commission regulation, $500.00;

(d) deer not included in subsection (1)(c), antelope not included in subsection (1)(c), fisher, raptor not included in subsection (1)(c), swan, bobcat, white sturgeon, river-dwelling grayling, and paddlefish, $300.00;

(e) fur-bearing animals, as defined in 87-2-101 and not listed in subsection (1)(c) or (1)(d), $100.00;

(f) game bird (except swan), $25.00;

(g) game fish, $10.00."

Fish and other Aquatics

Walls in pet shops are lined with tanks containing creatures from beneath the sea. The following sections address laws protecting these aquatic species.

5-34. Means of catching game fish generally.

"It shall be unlawful for any person to take, catch or kill or attempt to take, catch or kill any game fish by any other means than ordinary hook and line, artificial lure, troll or spinner in any of the public waters of this state. Any person who violates the provisions of this section shall be guilty of a misdemeanor and, on conviction, shall be punished by a fine of not less than $25.00 nor more than $100.00."

> Once again, the fine set out above was probably instituted when dinosaurs roamed the earth. Do not expect to see fines in amounts capable of causing a house payment to be missed.

5-35. Catching game or Non game fish by use of gill, trammel, etc., nets.

"(a) It shall be unlawful for any person to take, catch, capture or kill any game or non game fish by use of a gill, trammel or similar type net in any waters impounded by a dam, or constituting a reservoir. Whoever violates this subsection is guilty of a misdemeanor and, upon conviction, shall be punished as prescribed by law.

(b) It shall be unlawful for any person to take, catch, capture or kill any game or noontime fish by use of a gill, trammel or similar type net in any part of any river lying within the boundaries of the state and all tributaries thereto. Any person violating the provisions of this subsection shall be guilty of a misdemeanor and upon conviction, shall be punished by a fine or not less than $ 100.00 nor more than $500.00 or by imprisonment in the county jail for six months or by both such fine and imprisonment."

> Illegal methods of fish capture are as diverse as the mind of man. In the Caribbean, a bottle of bleach is opened underwater in a cave or hole, which causes lobsters and crabs to rush to the surface. Telephoning (an electrical charge to the water), dynamite, and entrance-only traps are just a few.

> There is some subliminal, paranormal feature about catching fish that seems to drive some men and women almost mad. It is akin to roulette and fortune telling. The most exemplary citizen can be reduced to an habitual offender when it comes to fishing.

5-36. Use of game fish for bait—Generally.

"It shall be unlawful for any person in the state to use any game fish for fish bait at any time."

5-37. Same—Use of sunfish.

"It shall be lawful to use the following species of the sunfish family for bait in the streams and waters of the state; bluegill, red ear sunfish, green sunfish and/or any other species of bream; provided, that nothing in this section shall be so construed as to allow any person to have in his possession any sunfish or bream in excess of the daily creel limit, regardless of size."

5-38. Laws Protecting Black Bass, Salmon, Walleye, Pike, Trout and Lake Trout.

Sale of Salmon, Trout and Black Bass

"A person shall not buy or sell a salmon, trout, lake trout, walleye, northern pike, muskellunge or black bass taken in this state, or imported from another state or country where sale of such fish is prohibited, except such fish reared in licensed propagation farms within the state."

"As used in the Fish and Wildlife Law:

(1) a. 'Fish' means all varieties of the super-class Pisces.

b. 'Food fish' means all species of edible fish and squid (cephalopoda)

c. 'Migratory fish of the sea' means both catadromous and anadromous species of fish which live a part of their life span in salt water streams and oceans.

d. 'Fish protected by law' means fish protected, by law or by regulations of the department, by restrictions on open seasons or on size of fish that may be taken.

e. Unless otherwise indicated, 'Trout' includes brook trout, brown trout, red-throat trout, rainbow trout and splake. 'Trout,' 'landlocked salmon,' 'black bass,' 'pickerel,' 'pike,' and 'walleye' mean respectively, the fish or groups of fish identified by those names, with or without one or more other common names of fish belonging to the group. "Pacific salmon" means coho salmon, chinook salmon and pink salmon."

f. trout, black bass, lake trout, landlocked salmon, muskellunge, pike, pickerel and walleye taken from fishing preserve waters licensed pursuant to section 11-1913."

5-39. Catching, etc., of fish in private ponds, lakes, pools or reservoirs.

"It is hereby made unlawful for any person to take, catch or kill or attempt to take, catch or kill fish or aid in the taking, catching or killing of fish or any species by the means or use of a seine, net, trap or any similar or other device which may be used for taking, catching, killing or stunning fish (other than by the use of hook and line, rod and reel) or by use of dynamite or other explosives or by the use of any poison, poisonous substance, fisheberries, lime or other deleterious or poisonous matter in any private pond, private lake, private pool or private reservoir of this state, except as otherwise specifically provided in the section."

> Only Adolph Hitler could have devised so very many illegal methods of taking fish.

> The Conservation Department simply must pass laws such as these regulating fishing. Some anglers have patience, experience, or know-how. Some have none of these, and some have all. But all fishermen (and women) are equally avid. If a fish attractor were found on Mt. Everest, the summit would be reduced to a hump in six months.

5-40. Saltwater Species.

"As used in this title, the term 'saltwater' shall include and mean all oysters, saltwater fish, saltwater shrimp, diamond back terrapin, sea turtle, crabs, lobster and other regulated species of marine or saltwater animal life existing or living in the water within the territorial jurisdiction of the coastal states."

5-41. Tax on terrapins caught, etc., for commercial purposes; minimum legal size; possession of undersized terrapins.

"A tax of $.05 is hereby laid on each turtle or terrapin packed, canned or caught for commercial purposes in this state or the waters within the territorial jurisdiction of this state. It shall be unlawful for any diamond back terrapin measuring less than six inches from the anterior to the posterior extremes of the body underneath to be caught or taken from the waters of the state, and any person having in his possession an undersized turtle shall be guilty of a misdemeanor."

> This statute was finally repealed by Federal preemption.

> During the Great Depression, turtles of all sorts were nearly hunted to extinction. The diamond back terrapin, found in the coastal southeastern states, had always been considered fine table food. Rather than prohibit a hungry population from enjoying a native delicacy, size limits were imposed. These limits persisted until preempted by Federal statute.

5-42. Crab catcher: license for use of more than five crab traps; rules and regulations.

"Any person taking crabs for commercial purposes or using more than five crab traps for person, noncommercial purposes must first obtain and have in possession a 'crab catcher's' license. The fee for said license shall be $50.00 and shall be paid to the Department of Conservation and Natural Resources."

> There are literally hundreds of species of crabs the world over. Maryland's blue crabs and San Francisco's Dungeness crabs are popular for their taste. Actually, crabs play a crucial role in marine ecology and life cycles. They are scavengers that keep carrion from polluting bays and gulfs.

5-43. Authority and procedure for leasing of bottoms in natural oyster reefs; cancellation and forfeiture of leases; disposition of proceeds from leases.

"In addition to the powers heretofore enumerated, the commissioner of conservation and natural resources shall have power to lease to any citizen of a coastal state or firm or corporation organized under the laws of the state and doing business within its limits, for the purpose of oyster culture, any bottom of the waters of the state in a natural oyster bed or reef in such areas and at such prices and under such conditions as he may determine. Such persons, firms or corporations desiring to avail themselves of the privileges of leasing oyster bottoms shall make application in writing to the commissioner of conservation and natural resources accompanied by such fee as may be prescribed by the commissioner of conservation and natural resources at the expense of the applicant, shall stake off the parcel to be leased, forwarding a description thereof to the commissioner of conservation and natural resources."

> A corresponding recent trend is to lease state oil and methane reserves to petroleum companies. Oysters are like canaries in a coal mine; they take in whatever is in the water and either signal the presence of pollutants when tested or die outright.

5-44. Inspection of oyster beds; closure order; relay of oysters from closed areas; promulgation of rules; penalty; enforcement.

"The state board of health is authorized to inspect waters of the state where oysters are grown and harvested. When the state health officer shall determine that the waters surrounding the oyster beds are unsafe for harvesting of said oysters, the state health officer shall issue an order to close the waters around said bed, which order shall be specific as to location of the area to be closed. After the issuance of such a closure order, no person shall harvest oysters in the said waters during the closure period. The state health officer is authorized to permit the department of conservation and natural resources to relay oysters from closed areas."

> Sadly, our statutes on oyster beds state that if they are found unsafe, they will be closed. Due to corporate indifference and rubber-stamp environmental protection agencies, our bays are so polluted with chemicals and coliform bacteria from overzealous developers that many beds have been closed almost continuously for two decades.

> Eating oysters on the half-shell is about as foolhardy as playing Russian roulette, due to water pollution, chemical run-off, and unregulated toxins.

5-45. Definitions, as respects Alabama, Georgia, Florida, Mississippi, Louisiana, South Carolina and Texas.

"For the purposes of this article, the following terms shall have the meanings described herein, unless the context otherwise requires:

(1) ALLIGATOR FARM. An enclosed area not located on public lands or waters, constructed so as to prevent the ingress and egress of alligators from surrounding public or private lands or waters and meeting other specifications prescribed by the department, where alligators are bred and raised under controlled conditions.

(2) ALLIGATOR FARMER. A person who raises alligators under controlled conditions which prohibit free movement of the animals onto and off of the farm or controlled area, and who may harvest alligators under the supervision of the department.

(3) ALLIGATOR PART. Any part of the carcass of an alligator, except its skin.

(4) ALLIGATOR PARTS DEALER. Any person who deals in alligator parts and who buys from an alligator farmer for the purpose of resale; or manufactures within the state alligator parts into a finished product; or purchases, cans, processes, or distributes alligator meat for wholesale or retail; provided, that a retailer selling canned alligator parts or a retailer purchasing alligator parts from an alligator parts dealer or a restaurant selling prepared alligator meat for human consumption shall not be classified as an alligator parts dealer."

> Federal laws have saved the alligator from virtually extinction and crippled illicit trade in alligator hides. The alligator population now flourishes (except in the Everglades where it is below normal). Alligator hides may be legally harvested and sold.

"Any person, firm, or corporation may engage in the business of propagating alligators on an alligator farm for propagation, and other commercial purposes by complying with the provisions of this article, and may thereafter sell either live alligators to other licensed alligator farmers only, or the parts or skins of such farm raised alligators to any person, for any purpose, including sale for food, either within or without this state."

> Regrettably, in order for an alligator to grow large enough to be eaten (ten years), it must have consumed a few thousand chickens. Could the alligator possibly be bypassed in this food chain?

5-46. Minimum weight of shrimp taken, etc., for commercial purposes; possession, sale, etc., of nonconforming shrimp.

"The commissioner of Conservation and Natural Resources shall set by regulation the minimum weight requirement of shrimp which are caught or taken from the territorial waters of coastal state for commercial purposes or which are brought into the state from waters beyond the territorial jurisdiction of the state for commercial purposes; provided, however, that such minimum weight requirements set by regulation of said commissioner of Conservation and Natural Resources shall require not more than a minimum number of shrimp with heads attached to weigh one pound and shall require not more than a minimum number of headless shrimp to the pound." (States vary as to the size of shrimp that may be kept. This is enforced by a state law setting forth the size mesh of the net).

> Years ago, I lived on the Dog River in Mobile, Alabama. Shrimp could be purchased off the docked shrimp boats for thirty cents a pound. At today's prices, thirty cents worth of shrimp would evaporate before it got to the refrigerator. When the shrimp are headed (the head is removed), the buyer loses one-third of his pound or package.

5-47. Hardship gill net license; renewal and transfer.

"(a) The Department of Conservation and Natural Resources shall immediately approve the hardship licenses selected on a certain date.

(b) An individual approved pursuant to subsection (a) shall be subject to the same renewal qualifications as persons licensed under the customary regulations.

(c) Hardship licenses approved by this section shall be subject to the transfer system established by the Department of Conservation and Natural Resources."

> States have softened the effect of bans on commercial fishing for salmon, cod and other "fished out" species by allowing lifetime fishermen to continue in their trade.

5-48. Live bait shrimp dealers license.

"Before any person, firm, or corporation engages in the taking, catching, transporting, or selling of live saltwater shrimp or other live bait for commercial bait purposes, he or she shall have in his or her possession a live bait shrimp dealer's license."

> Surely the reader has noticed by now that for a fisherman to be able to keep all the various and sundry licenses necessary to his livelihood, his billfold must be carried in a wheelbarrow.

5-49. Catching, etc., of shrimp; place and time.

"Licensed live bait catcher boats may take or catch, or attempt to take or catch, bait shrimp of any size in waters of the state in certain areas not permanently closed to shrimping. Licensed live bait catchers may take or catch, or attempt to take or catch, shrimp from 4:00 a.m. until 10:00 p.m. in areas closed to commercial shrimping."

> As the shrimper's day gets closer and closer to 10:00 p.m., the weary seaman notices that his catch contains many nocturnal sea creatures such as mantis shrimp, eels, and phosphoric creatures which glow green.

5-50. Catching, etc. of shrimp by persons with recreational boat shrimping license; manner of taking; limitation on quantities taken.

"Persons with a recreational boat shrimping license may use a trawl having a width of 16 feet or less as measured at the cork line to catch, or attempt to catch, saltwater shrimp for bait or noncommercial purposes not to exceed five gallons of shrimp per person per day only at the same time and in the waters open to commercial shrimping."

> Along the Gulf Coast, recreational shrimping is conducted in time intervals, such as a three-beer troll or a six-pack troll.
>
> Florida's law on net mesh size permits the capture of smaller shrimp than Alabama's. Texas, Georgia, Mississippi, and Louisiana require approximately the same size mesh.

5-51. Rivers, bayous and creeks permanently closed; areas designed as exclusive bait shrimping areas.

"All rivers, bayous, and creeks of the state are permanently closed to the taking of saltwater shrimp for any purpose."

> There is no need to break this law by shrimping in rivers or creeks. On the opening day of shrimp season, boats have actually been known to sink under the weight of overfilled nets in the legal water of the bays. In Louisiana, shrimping in canals and bays is done with a type of net unique to France and the Scandinavian countries. It is called a butterfly net, and is used at night to skim the surface, where shrimp congregate under cover of darkness.

5-52. Lobster—Maine or Spiny

> The taking or trapping of Maine lobster (those from northern waters, with claws) and spiny lobster (from tropical or warm waters, without claws) is intensely regulated, and enforced for purposes of preservation and propagation. These creatures enjoy protection due to their membership in the food chain, not the dignity of their species.

Lobsters; permit to take; prohibited acts.

"1. Any person domiciled within the state may take and land lobsters (Homarus americanus) from the waters of the state or land lobsters in the state taken elsewhere upon first obtaining a permit."

A further regulation states that:

"(1) Lobsters in spawn shall not be taken or possessed at any time. Eggs shall not be removed from such lobsters.

(2) The landing or possession of lobster or parts thereof not in the shell, detached lobster tails or claws, or any other part of a lobster that has been separated from the lobster is prohibited. This prohibition applies to any lobster men licensed by the state.

(3) The landing or possession of any V-notched female lobster is prohibited. This prohibition applies to any lobster men licensed by the state and to marine and coastal district food fish and crustacean dealers and shippers license holders. V-notched female lobster shall mean any female lobster bearing a V-shaped notch (i.e. a straight-sided triangular cut without setal hairs, at least one-quarter inch in depth and tapering to a sharp point) in the flipper next to the right of the center flipper as viewed from the rear of the female lobster. V-notched female lobster also means any female which is mutilated in a manner which could hide, obscure or obliterate such a mark. The right flipper will be examined when the underside of the lobster is down and have the authority to adopt by rule or regulation a modified definition of 'V-notched female lobster' to reflect any changes to the definition the Atlantic States Marine Fisheries Commission may adopt."

> Lobsters found in Florida waters and throughout the Caribbean are akin to the South African rock lobster. Florida, the Bahamas, and islands in the Windward and Leeward chains observe laws as to season, limit, size, and females with eggs. In the Turks and Caicus islands, even out of season, one "can take as many as he needs for a meal." In Mexico and Cuba, such laws are generally ignored. Vacationing tourists and divers disavow any knowledge of seasons or limits. As a result, the spiny lobster decreases in number year after year.

5-53. Charge for buying or otherwise obtaining freshwater mussels; disposition of revenues; violation as a misdemeanor.

"Any person, firm or corporation who purchases or otherwise obtains freshwater mussels taken from state waters shall pay to the Department of Conservation and Natural Resources Game and Fish Division the amount equal to $0.05 per pound of mussel shells, with or without meat, purchased or obtained."

> The great bulk of the mussel harvest is exported to Japan—the shells, that is. What the Japanese do with these shells is a great mystery. I suspect the shells, extruded or pulverized, wind up on store shelves in the U.S. as some other product.

Epilogue

At this point in time, it can be said that our examination of the law has consisted of the broad application of needs, wants, protections, liabilities, defenses, and requirements which rather uniformly define and determine the laws on pets and animals in those United States.

A sequitur, that is, a matter that must logically follow, is this question: where in the continuum of space and time does our evolving body of laws correspond to the effort, apathy and/or resistance to animal rights that has existed on this planet for the four hundred years' prevalence of the written word?

Consider if you will the subjects of animal rights and animal laws as a two-tiered horizon. One tier is inhabited by more progressive persons who consider the rights of animals as innate, that is, predestined by the natural order of the universe as it provides for all its living inhabitants.

The other tier consists of persons who view animals as having only those rights that are bestowed upon them by humankind.

It is my belief and strong conviction that the progressive view of animals will ultimately become humanity's resolved view of its cotenants on the planet.

Great Britain is light-years ahead of the United States in its recognition of the rights of animals. However, Great Britain is not a single voice crying out in the wilderness, if one considers the many other countries in the world.

In order that the reader may be aware of the tremendous human forces supportive of genuinely coequal rights for animals, a summarization of various worldwide movements are mentioned here. Of some importance is the reader's cognizance that many of these groups or forces adamantly follow Dr. Martin Luther King Jr.'s statement from his 1964 book, *Why We Can't Wait*, that "An individual who breaks a law that conscience tells him is unjust, and who willingly accepts the penalty of imprisonment in order to arouse the conscience of the community over its injustice, is in reality expressing the highest respect for the law."

Not to mention the ASPCA, PETA, or Greenpeace, one group that is quite proactive is The Animal Liberation Front (ALF). Encouraged by the boldness and effectiveness of ALF, a New Zealand organization named the New Zealand Antivivisection Society (NZAVS) has become similarly vocal and formulative

NZAVS originally followed conventional legal channels as it sought to establish a higher order of rights for animals. Petitions to parliament and other means were said to have been blocked. At that point, NZAVS adopted ALF's more radical actions under that organization's name. Allow me to recount some of the goals and activities of that organization.

NZAVS endeavors to work legally and peacefully to educate the public about the dangers of vivisection (the surgical exploitation of living animals in the "name" of research). NZAVS recognizes, however, that "...direct actions that liberate laboratory animals or cause economic damage to vivisectors often gain more publicity and educate the public more than the most spectacular legal protest marches or rallies that are, with few exceptions ignored by the mass media."

Other groups that champion animal rights include Nottingham Rainbow Centers, a British society that promotes vegetarianism and closely monitors the voting records of the members of parliament on such matters as the abolishment of fox hunting, fur farming, and deer hunting.

The Universities Federation for Animal Welfare (UFAW) was founded in 1926 as the University of London Animal Welfare Society. Their history of accomplishments is diverse. In their first year of existence, they began a nationwide campaign to ban the gin (steel) trap. They also created humane methods of killing whales, dogs and crustaceans. In 1946 they began the Nature Conservancy. They produced, in that same year, a laboratory manual detailing procedures for the humane dissection of animals.

By 1966, the UFAW had procured protection for seals and otters. In 1986, the UFAW established worldwide criteria that led to better treatment of zoo animals. The years 1992 to 2000 witnessed the creation of scholarships by UFAW that support research study and animal welfare.

In comparison, United States citizens might well be surprised to learn that nine northeastern states (Connecticut, Massachusetts, Maine, New Hampshire, New Jersey, New York, Pennsylvania, Rhode Island, and Vermont) are home to no less than fifty-one animal rescue foundations. These organizations, with names ranging from Animal Angels Rescue Foundation to The Last Post—a retirement community for pets whose owners have died—are but the iceberg's tip of such groups worldwide.

Although this survey of animal rights groups seems to paint a picture of optimism and prospect with a broad brush, what is best for the whole of the animal kingdom might, on occasion, be a curse for a single pet or its owner.

Individuals (and organizations) rail against the harshness of Britain's requirement that pets and animals from non-European Union countries be quarantined for six months. This is the world's most stringent anti-rabies program. An article from the London Times (22 June 2001) recounts how President George W. Bush's newly appointed ambassador to Great Britain, William Farish, sent his dog (with its keeper) to an upscale kennel in France for four months (the quarantine requirement for E.U. countries). He did this in order to allow the animal to elude the possible negative health effects that the British quarantine might have imposed.

As responsive to animal rights as Britain unquestionably is, the United States responded more quickly than any other world power to an international Fur and Leather Show held in Beijing in 1985. Businessmen from seventeen countries attended, including Japan, the U.S., Great Britain, and Canada. Upon learning that the garments presented were made of mink, wolf, raccoon, cat, dog, and sheep fur, the United States Congress passed the Dog and Cat Protection Act of 1999 (S. 1197, 106th Congress).

The African Convention on the Conservation of Nature and Natural Resources was the offshoot of an international agreement to conserve wild animals, birds, and fish in Africa. This assembly first took place in 1900, and the compact was revised in 1933. An agreement to agree is hardly a control measure, however, and it can be argued that more animals on that continent have perished in the century since the convention than in the prior two millennia.

Despite a plethora of treaties, conventions, and agreements (all twentieth-century protectionist phenomena), forests are cut, habitats bulldozed, and insecticides used with impunity. At the time of this writing, Nicaraguan cargo ships are transporting sea turtles to Japan; swamps in Africa are being drained for garden plots, endangering the native slender-nosed crocodiles; and Indonesian farmers liberally use DDT, despite its long-term effects on entire species of exotic birds.

Have elephants been saved? Studies show that country-by-country bans on ivory imports are unenforceable. Because Japan did not impose a ban on its own imports, the ivory supply that might previously have gone to the U.S., England, or France instead makes its way to Japan.

Oil slicks from Desert Storm, still floating in the Gulf of Bahrain, will destroy shrimp, fish, dolphins, and plankton for at least twenty more years, according to Britain's Royal Society for the Prevention of Cruelty to Animals.

Animal cloning is a perfected phenomenon, and human cloning is sure to follow (illegally). Where will genetic boundaries then be drawn between animals and people?

That all the world is not predisposed to support ecology and animal rights was (uncharacteristically) seen in Great Britain, where Dave Morris and Helen Steel were sued by McDonald's for publishing a leaflet entitled "What's Wrong With McDonalds: Everything They Don't Want You to Know." After a trial that lasted nearly a year, McDonalds was vindicated of the leaflets' charges of mistreating animals and destroying rain forests. The authors of those leaflets will be paying legal costs for years and years.

On a brighter note, however, The United States Supreme Court, in an opinion submitted upon a question from the Tennessee Valley authority (S.C. #94-859, June, 1995), stated that harm to a habitat includes habitat modification. This is a noteworthy advance in a world of megacorporations that offer to duplicate wetlands, when million-year-old wetland sites are being drained for the construction of a retail mammoth pursuing some location-saturation gimmick.

In the final analysis, there are persons and groups worldwide seeking greater protection for animals and habitats, as well as force of law to guarantee and enforce those protections. On the same global scale, however, we have persons, groups, countries, and alliances that oppose such protections due to centuries old myths, selfish intransigency, and the dreaded juggernaut of profit.

1. We have been taught, time and again, that there is strength in numbers.

2. We have learned that we cannot become too familiar with our subject.

3. We have learned the necessity of walking a mile in the shoes of those who oppose us.

4. And, finally, we have learned that it is the squeaking wheel that will cause the driver to stoop and attend to the noisy condition.

Like the canaries in the coal mines, what is bad for animals is usually bad for humans. Efforts to save the canary have often saved man. Should this work serve some lasting purpose, even if no greater than to free a sparrow skyward so that it might salute its right to life, then I will tearfully take Judicial Notice of a foundation having been laid upon the dust of a million pets and animals gone before that will serve as a refuge for the remainder left to inhabit the world with us.

CONCLUSION

This book, *It's the Law: Pets, Animals, and the Law* cannot truly come to a conclusion, for the recognition of the rights and dignity of animals increases with each passing day.

Further, the deponent sayeth not.

GLOSSARY

Abandoned animal An animal whose owner has voluntarily relinquished possession of it with intention of terminating his ownership, but without vesting it in another. Specifically, an animal whose owner cannot be found after reasonable effort and legal notice. The one taking up an abandoned animal may secure rights of possession or ownership.

Animal shelter A humane society, animal welfare authority, municipal or county pound whose statutory duty is to collect and maintain abandoned, unlicensed or abused animals and return to owner, let out for adoption or dispose of said animals.

Animal therapy A form of medical care by which long term health care facilities utilize the presence of pets, especially dogs or cats to be in the presence of patients, offering the elements of caring, affection or amusement for the patients' general well-being.

Animal Welfare Act A Federal law, specifically US Public Law 91-579, which mandates standards of minimum care, keeping, and nutrition in the areas of animal sales, transportation, breeding, etc.

Arbitration	A legal alternative to a jury trial, wherein, by prior agreement or statute, the parties to a contract, wherein a dispute has arisen, submit the controversy to a panel of neutral arbitrators for a usually quicker, non-appealable resolution.
Barbiturate	Any of the group of barbituric acid derivatives used in medicine as a sedative or hypnotic. Most states require an overdose of barbiturate or some similar central nervous system depressant as a required method of euthanizing terminally ill or unwanted animals.
Brute	Non human creature; beast. A term used in some state codes to define an animal or pest.
Burning, cauterization	An illegal deception employed to alter or disguise the true age of a horse, mule or other soliped, by causing the proximal tooth surfaces to reveal less wear.
Canid	Any carnivorous mammal of the Canidae family, which includes foxes, wolves, dogs, jackals, and coyotes
Canine	Of or like a dog; pertaining to or characteristic of dogs.
Certificate of registration	Documentary evidence of compliance with state law requiring proof of ownership of a particular animal or object.
Choking disease	An equine disease most likely related to tuberculosis; highly contagious and ultimately terminal.

Cockpit	A pit or enclosed place where cockfights (rooster males) are held.
Commercial dog breeder	A person or corporation that engages in the propagation of a species for sale and profit.
Common law	The system of law originating in England, as distinct from the civil or Roman law and the canon or ecclesiastical law.
Coydog	The hybrid offspring of a coyote and a feral dog.
Deadfall	An illegal and cruel type of trap in which a weight falls and crushes the prey. This is often used on larger animals.
Dipping	An equine, bovine or porcine method of parasite control required by most states to prevent and control diseases spread by ticks.
Discretion of the court	Power or privilege of the court (judge) to act unhampered by legal rule or jury vote.
Docking	A method of cutting and breaking the tail of a horse so as to give it an arch at its nexus to the rump.
Domitae naturae	Tame; domesticated; not wild. Applied to domestic animals in which a man may have absolute property.
ECFVG	Educational Commission for Foreign Veterinarian Graduates—Graduates of a foreign school of veterinary medicine may furnish proof of an ECFVG certificate and then sit for the National Board Examination.

Equine	Of or resembling a horse; having four legs with single, not cloved, hoofs.
Estray	A domestic animal, as a horse, cow or sheep found wandering or without an owner.
Euthanasia	The act of putting to death, painlessly, an animal suffering from an incurable disease or not being claimed or wanted by an person.
Exposed	Having been seized with teeth or claws by an animal exposed to rabies.
Feline, felid	Belonging or pertaining to the cat family.
Felony	A crime of a graver or more atrocious nature than those designated as misdemeanor; involving moral turpitude (inherent baseness or vileness).
Ferae naturae	Of a wild nature or disposition; lacking the capacity of temperament to be docile.
Feral	Existing in a natural state, or having reverted to the wild state.
Fiduciary	A person who stands in a special relation of trust, confidence, or responsibility in certain obligations to others, such as one who administers a trust.
Glanders	A contagious disease chiefly of horses and mules, but communicable to man; caused by *Acinobaccillus mallei;* characterized by swollen glands and profuse mucous discharge from the nostrils.

Glycol	Ethylene glycol or any alcohol containing two hydroxyl groups. Used in antifreeze, its sweet taste appeals to animals—which is why is as used as a poison. Even a small dose is lethal.
Good Samaritan	In the context of medical care rendered by a licensed veterinarian to an injured animal; emergency treatment rendered by a veterinarian, who volunteers to render treatment out of concern, not by contract, whereby the veterinarian may not be held liable for any poor result or mistake.
Grandfather clause	A provision in a regulatory or prohibitionary statute, allowing persons who have been practicing or engaging in an endeavor to continue, despite the general application of the law.
Guide Dog	A specially trained, licensed dog whose acquired expertise allows it access to whatever places and accommodations its blind master should frequent.
Hardship license	An exception to a general prohibition on an occupation or activity; the restricted right to continue an occupation despite a general ban.
Homestead exemption	A specific statutory value or amount of personal property, including pets, which are exempt or free from judgment or levy.
Humane	The character of caring; as in the purpose of an animal humane society in caring for, placing out for adoption, or painlessly euthanizing animals.

Immunization	An injection of anti-rabies (or other) serum into a pet or animal to prevent the occurrence of rabies (or other disease) if the animal is bitten or seized.
Impounding officer	An agent of a county, state or municipal animal control authority who sees to the impoundment of loose or abandoned animals.
Invitee	One who is on the premises of an owner—private or commercial by express or implied invitation.
Jack	The male of the family of equine, known as donkey or ass.
Jennet	A female ass or donkey; also a small Spanish horse.
Judge of Probate	The county or borough judge referred to variously as judge of common pleas, judge of district court, justice of the peace; the inferior county court.
Jurisdiction	The power of a state, through its courts or enforcement officers to take legally effective action.
Justification	The maintaining or showing, in court, of sufficient reason why the defendant did what he is called upon to answer.
Leash law	Municipal or county ordinance requiring that animals kept within city or corporate limits be enclosed or contained form running loose; when off the owner's premises, the animal is to be kept on a leash.

Licensed	The class of persons required to obtain a license from the state to carry on a business or do an activity that the state regulates.
Lien	A charge, security or encumbrance on property (in this case, an animal) securing payment of a debt, charge or duty.
Maim	To cripple or mutilate in any way; an illegal disabling or disfiguring.
Malicious	Characterized by, or involving malice; done with wicked or mischievous motives.
Mayhem	Unlawfully and violently depriving an animal (in this case) of the use of its members in order to render it less able to defend itself.
Misdemeanor	Offenses lower than felonies and generally those punishable by fine or imprisonment other than in a penitentiary and for no longer than 365 days.
Mitigation	Alleviation; abatement or diminution of a penalty or punishment imposed by law.
Nuisance	That which annoys and disturbs one in possession of his property; rendering its ordinary use or occupation physically uncomfortable to him. A nuisance may be a civil action sued on by an individual or criminal violation prosecuted by the district attorney. A nuisance may be private, affecting only one or an identifiable group. A public nuisance affects the public at large and is prosecuted by the district attorney or attorney general.

Open range	A tract or district of land within which domestic animals in large numbers range for subsistence. The term is used on the Great Plains of the United States.
Pet therapy	A newly recognized method of care and enhancement of general well being afforded to patients in hospitals and long term health care facilities, whereby a pet or pets is allowed on the premises for the comfort, affection and/or amusement of patients.
Possession	The actual holding or keeping, either with or without rights of ownership.
Preceptor	A veterinary student, intern or assistant, working under the control and responsibility of a licensed veterinarian.
Prima facie	On the face of it; a fact presumed to be true unless disproved by some evidence to the contrary.
Psittacine	A parrot or similar bird capable of imitating sounds or speech.
Rabid	Having contracted the infectious disease rabies (*Formido inexoribilis*); dogs, cats, other animals and man may suffer fatal results without treatment; also known as hydrophobia.
Range laws	A body of laws that has been enacted by state legislatures in the states of the Great Plains as well as by the U.S. Department of the Interior. These laws drew their content from the novelty and experience of using the open range.

Rebuttable presumption	A presumption is an inference of the truth or falsity of any fact drawn by probable reasoning. A rebuttable presumption is an inference that may be rebutted or disproved by contradictory evidence.
Riparian	Pertaining to the banks of a river or navigable waterway. Ownership of land abutting a waterway bestows certain riparian rights.
Seizor	The person or entity that puts or invests itself with possession; may include legal possession, which is possession with ownership or title.
Sentient	A term used to define pets or animals by some legislatures, meaning having the power of perception by the senses.
Shoat	A young pig.
Soliped	Broad generalization of horses, mules, asses, donkeys, etc.; meaning to have a solid or single hoof, as opposed to a cloved hoof.
Spay	To remove the ovaries of an animal in order to prevent further breeding.
State code	A complete system or compilation of the existing laws of a state, arranged into chapters, subheads, table of contents and index.
Stud service	The fee or reimbursement (one of the offspring) charged by the owner of a male animal kept for breeding. One early definition of the word "stud" means "to spread or scatter".

Superannuated	Too old for use, work or service.
Theriogenology	The study or analysis of the breed or lineage of an animal.
Title	Evidence of right which a person has to a thing; more than mere possession, it is ownership.
Thoroughbred	A purebred or pedigreed animal, especially a horse.
Tort	Damage, injury, or a wrongful act done willfully, negligently, or in circumstances involving strict liability, but not involving breach of contract, for which a civil suit can be brought.
Toxicologist	A professionally educated specialist dealing with the science of the effects, antidotes, detection and analysis of poisons.
Trust	A trust is a legal instrument drawn or declared by a party for the benefit of another party or entity. In almost all state codes, a person may provide benefits to an animal or animals for a specified period, in trust.
Veterinarian	A licenses, trained professional who specializes in the branch of medicine dealing with the study, prevention and treatment of animal diseases.
Vicious animal	An animal possessed of the tendency or propensity to do any act which might endanger the person or property of another. This legal appellation may be derived from previous behavior or class.

Wanton	Acts or behavior characterized by extreme recklessness, foolhardiness, or reckless disregard for the rights or safety of another. A degree of culpability under the law which is greater than negligence (accidental) but lesser than willful (intentional).
Wolf-dog hybrid	The offspring of the union of a wolf (family is *Canis lupus*) and a dog, usually German Shepherd. This hybrid has mainly resulted from purposeful efforts to create a breed but also from random breeding in the wild. Almost all states have laws permitting citizens and officials to kill or capture a wolf-dog hybrid, under certain circumstances.

State Statutes

As stated in the text, the subject matter and wording of over half the states' statutes on pets and animals are essentially uniform in scope.

In those instances, statutes cited as exemplary have been those of Alabama, the situs of the writer's judicial office.

	Page	Statute
Chapter 1	14	Conn. Gen. St. T. 22 s. 344
	15	Conn. Gen. St. T. 22 s. 344(d)
	17	Ill. T. 7 s. 3907
	18	Ark. T -7-97
	19	Ca. Penal St. 5971
	20	Conn. Gen. St. 7. 22 s. 344 (a)
	21	Ariz. Code 44 -1799.04
	22	Ark. Code Ann. T. 4-97-107
	24	Ariz. Code 44-1799.05
	26	Ariz. Code 44-1799.06
	18	Ariz. Code 44-1799.07
	29	Pa. St. 3 P.S.A. 459-206
	31	Ark. Code 1-6-115
	32	Mass. St. 272 s. 80A
	32	U.S. Pub. Law 91-579
	33	Va. St. s. 3.1-796.93:1
	34	Ariz. St. s. 5-104
	35	Pa. St. 35 P.S.A. 448.821
	36	Hi. St. s. 322-51
	36	Ariz. St. s. 36-1409.01

	38	Ca. Health Stat. 19901
	39	Ca. Civil s. 798.33
	40	Ariz. 14-2907
	41	Ca. Rev & Tax s. 224
Chapter 2	44	Al. Code T. 3-1-2
	46	Al. Code T. 3-7A-4
	46	Al. Code T. 3-7A-5
	47	Al. Code T. 3-7A-7
	47	Al. Code T. 3-7A-8
	48	Al. Code T. 3-7A-9
	49	Wy. St. s. 11-31-301
	51	Al. Code T. 13A-11-150
	51	Al. Code T. 21-7-9
	52	Ct. St. s. 22-344 (b)
	53	Ma. St. 272 s. 80A
	53	Ma. St. Ch. 752.61
	54	Co. St. s. 35-80-102
	56	Al. Code T. 34-29-90
	57	Al. Code T. 11-65-39
	58	7 USCA s. 2131
	59	Al. Code T. 13A-12-200.1
	60	Al. T. 13A-12-5
	63	Al. Code 13A-12-5
Chapter 3	66	Al. Code T. 3-1-5
	67	Va. St. s. 3.1-796.95
	68	Al. Code T. 3-1-5
	69	Al. Code T. 3-6-2
	70	Al. Code T. 3-6-3
	72	Mt. St. 7-23-2109
	73	Al. Code T. 3-1-3
	75	Al. Code T. 3-1-6
	77	Oh. St. s. 955.11
	78	Al. Code T. 3-1-2
	79	Al. Code 13A-11-14
	80	Al. Code 3-1-13

Chapter 4		
	83	Al. Code 3-1-8
	85	Al. Code 13A-11-14
	86	Al. Code 3-1-29
	90	Al. Code 3-1-10
	92	Al. Code 3-4-2
	93	Al. Code 3-4-4
	94	Al. Code 3-5-2
	95	Al. Code 3-5-5
	95	Al. Code T. 6-5-337
	96	Al. Code 2-15-113
	96	Al. Code 2-15-44
	96	Al. Code 3-2-1
	97	Al. Code 3-2-2
	97	Al. Code 3-3-1
	98	Al. Code 2-15-22
	98	Al. Code 2-15-24
	99	Al. Code 2-15-296
	100	Al. Code 2-15-298
	100	Al. Code 2-16-7
	100	Fla. St. 775-082
	101	Al. Code T. 2-15-211
	102	Al. Code 2-15-231
	102	Al. Code 13A-12-4
	102	Al. Code 25-9-153
	103	Al. Code 25-9-83
	104	Al. Code 22-10-1
	104	Al. Code 22-23-47
	105	Al. Code 32-5A-5
	105	Al. Code 32-5-248
	106	Al. Code 35-11-330
	107	Al. Code T. 35-11-70
	109	Al. Code 3-1-20
	109	Al. Code 3-1-21
	110	Al. Code 3-1-25
	110	Al. Code 3-1-27

	110	Al. Code 3-1-28
	111	Al. Code 22-20-9
	112	Al. Code 36-18-2
Chapter 5	114	NY Envir. 11-1721
	115	Ark. St. s. 16-35.010
	116	Ark. St. T. 15-4-46
	119	Al. Code T. 9-11-235
	120	Al. Code 9-11-236
	121	Al. Code 9-11-237
	122	Al. Code 9-11-238
	122	Al. Code 9-11-239
	123	Al. Code 9-11-250
	123	Al. Code 9-11-251
	124	Ok. St. T. 29 s. 5-411
	125	Al. Code T. 9-11-244
	126	Mn. s. T. 97b-641
	127	Al. Code T. 9-11-340
	127	Al. Code 9-11-412
	127	Al. Code 9-11-410
	127	Al. Code 9-11-375
	128	Al. Code 9-11-417
	129	Al. Code 9-11-418
	129	Al. Code 9-11-430
	130	Al. Code 9-11-431
	130	Al. Code 9-11-432
	130	Al. Code 9-11-52
	131	Al. Code 9-11-305
	131	Al. Code 9-11-306
	132	Al. Code 9-11-262
	132	Al. Code 9-11-264
	133	Al. Code 9-11-16
	133	Al. Code 9-11-265
	134	Al. Code 9-11-265
	135	Al. Code 9-2-13
	135	Vt. St. T. 10 App. s. 33

135	Al. Code T. 9-1-87
138	Al. Code 9-11-88
139	Al. Code 9-11-89
141	NY Envir. s. 11-0103
143	Vt. St. T. 10 s. 4611
144	NY Envir. s. 11-0103
145	Al. Code T. 9-12-124
146	Al. Code 9-12-126
147	Al. Code 9-12-200
148	Al. Code 9-12-46
149	Al. Code 9-12-123.1
150	Al. Code 9-12-54.1
150	Al. Code 9-12-54.1
151	Al. Code 9-12-54.5
152	Al. Code 9-12-54.6
153	NY Envir. s. 13-0329

INDEX

A

Alligator 2, 136, 147
Animal
　abandoned 81
　defined 16
　food 20
　neglected or abused 80
　protected, hunting of 120
　vicious or dangerous 73
　wild, unprotected 116
Animal research facilities 23, 51 - 52
　and wild animals 114
Animal rights
　efforts in U.S. 157
　international efforts 155
Animal Welfare Act, Federal 32
Animals, food 21
Anti-cruelty laws 61
　for exhibitions 60
Anti-obscenity laws 59
Apartment, pets in 30
Arbitration 25
Armadillo 137

B

Baiting, of protected species 125
Bankruptcy, and pets 40
Bans, municipal, on breeds 33
Bear 60, 124, 140
　wrestling 61

Beaver
　bounty on 133
　trapping of 133
Birds, protected, hunting of 120
Bobcat 2, 116, 137 - 138
Branding
　illegal, penalty for 110
　registration of 98
Breeders, licensure of 14
Buffalo 115, 138, 140

C

Canine corps dog 44, 51
Cats, feral 2, 47 - 48, 137, 163
Cemeteries, pet 38
Coalmines, animals in 102
Cockfighting 102
Conservation, international efforts 158
Cougar 119
Coydog 33
Coyote 116, 136, 140
Crabs, licensure to catch 145
Cropping, of dog's ears 31
Cruelty, criminal penalties for 83
Cruelty prevention officers 79

D

Deer, legal and illegal hunting of 122
Defenses
    for injury to livestock 90
    for owner, in civil action 72
Docking, of horse's tail 31
Dog fighting 86
Dog racing 34
Dog, dangerous 33
Domitae naturae 9

E

Estray 93, 96
Euthanasia, of pets 19, 81

F

Felony, defined 88
Fences
    for livestock 92
    for pets 66
Ferae naturae 9, 74, 138
Fish
    game, catching of 141
    illegal methods of capture 142
    non-game, catching of 141
    protected 143
Food animals, killing of 20
Fox 119
Free bite 9, 67 - 68, 70, 72

G

Game, laws, enforcement of 129
Game, protected, types 124
Glanders 108
Greyhound, adoption programs for 34
Guide dogs 53

H

Horsemeat, sale of 122
Hunting dog, regulation of 132

I

Importation, of species,
    regulation of 135
Impoundment 51
Insurance, health, for pets 41
Invitee 70

K

Kennels, licensure of 14

L

Leash laws 67
Liability
    civil 76
    criminal 73
Liability of owner
    and confined pet 69
    and livestock 94
    and unconfined pet 68
    in equine activities 95
License
    for pet sitting 31
    hunting 127
    hunting dog trainer's 131
Livestock
    defined 92
    wanton or malicious injury of 90
Lobster, regulations on catching 151
Lynx 140

M

Misdemeanor, defined 88
Mobile home parks, pets in 38
Mountain lion 124, 140
Mussels, regulations on commercial use 153

N

Nuisance
    private 73
    public 71, 104

O

Oysters, regulations on collection of 146

P

Permittee 70
Pet, defined 16
Pet shop
    conditions 21, 23
    defined 15, 17
    licensure 14
    maintenance of 18
    regulation of 17
    return policies 24
    signage in 15
Pet sitting 31
Poisoning, of livestock and wildlife 112
Presumption, rebuttable 27
Probate, and pets 40
Public housing, pets in 36

Q

Quail 127

R

Rabbits, baby, restrictions 100
Rabies
    animal exposed to 51
    defined 44
    exposure 44
    immunization 46
    nonimmunization of pet 47
    owner liability 78
    quarantine 45, 49
    redeeming pet without tag 48
    tags 46
Racing, horse or dog 58
Range laws 93
Restriction, numerical 27, 30

S

Salmonella 62
Saltwater species, defined 144
Seeing eye dog 51
Shrimp, regulations on catching 148
Stud service, livestock 106

T

Taxation, pets exempt from 40
Teeth, tampering with, of horse or mule 109
Theft, of property, penalty for 59
Therapy, animal or pet 35
Tiger 140
Tilapia 137
Title
    to livestock 98
    to pets 86
Toxicologist, legal duties of 112
Trapping, regulations on 133
Trusts, for pets 39
Turkey, wild 121, 138
Turtles 62
    commercial use regulated 145

V

Vehicle, animal-drawn 105
Veterinary medicine
    and abandoned animals 57
    and Good Samaritan Act 57
    practice of 54
Vicious or dangerous animal
    control of 77
    dog 33
    legal killing of 77, 79
    owner liability for 73

W

Waterfowl, migratory, hunting of 130
Wells, abandoned, security of 40
Wild birds, protected and unprotected 114
Wildlife, ownership and possession of 138
Wolf 33, 76, 116, 136, 140, 158
    bounty on 117
    red 137
Wolf hybrid, right to kill 78
Wolverine 119, 140